the Natio
for Sc
a place fo

C000259002

GUIDE TO WALKS IN THE
NORTH-WEST
HIGHLANDS

the National Trust
for Scotland
a place for everyone

GUIDE TO WALKS IN THE
NORTH-WEST
HIGHLANDS
CHRIS TOWNSEND

Aurum

First published 2007 by Aurum Press Ltd
25 Bedford Avenue, London WC1 3AT

ISBN-10 1 84513 067 7
ISBN-13 978 1 84513 067 1

Book design by Robert Updegraff
Printed and bound in Italy by Printer Trento Srl

Cover photograph: **View over Loch na h-Airigh Fraoich to Suilven.**
Half-title photograph: **The north-west face of Ben Loyal from Ribigill.**
Title page photograph: **Looking north to Quinag from Suilven.**

Contents

Introduction   9

The Walks   19

1 Garbh Bheinn of Ardgour   20

2 Loch Shiel and the Coire Ghiubhsachain Hills   24

3 The South Shore of Loch Hourn   30

4 The Circuit of Beinn Fhada   36

5 The Falls of Glomach   44

6 Around Loch Affric   50

7 Beinn Bhan of Applecross   54

8 Through the Coulin Forest: Achnashellach to Torridon   58

9 Coire Mhic Fhearchair of Beinn Eighe   64

10 The Mountain Trail and Meall a'Ghiubhais   68

11 Peaks of the Flowerdale Forest   73

12 The Heights of Kinlochewe and Gleann Bianasdail   78

13 Cul Mor and Knockan Crag   84

14 Around the Cam Loch   90

15 Suilven   96

16 Quinag   104

17 The Splendid Falls of Coul   110

18 Foinaven   116

19 Ben Loyal   122

20 Sandwood Bay and Cape Wrath   129

21 Marsco   136

22 Loch Coruisk and the Elgol Coast Walk   140

23 South Duirinish and Moonen Bay Coastal Walk   144

24 The Quiraing   150

Useful Information   155

The National Trust for Scotland   156

Accommodation   156

Transport   157

Tourist Information Centres   157

Weather forecasts   158

Further reading   158

Glossary of Gaelic and Scots words   159

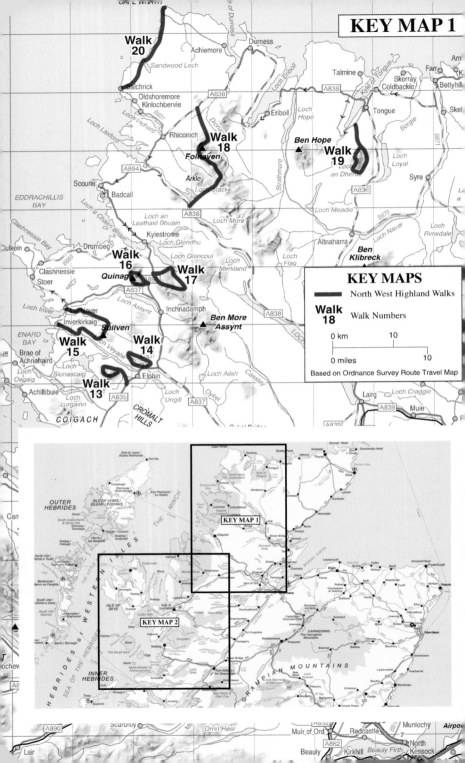

Introduction

The North-west Highlands covers all the land lying north and west of the Great Glen, the massive cleft that splits the Highlands from coast to coast, plus the Isle of Skye, which is now permanently attached to the mainland by the bridge at the Kyle of Lochalsh. This is a land of superlatives, with magnificent mountains in a wild array of shapes, the highest waterfalls and biggest sea cliffs in Britain, beautiful long lochs – both sea and freshwater – spectacular golden beaches, some of the oldest rocks in the world, ancient woodlands and much more, all intertwined to form a wonderful connected whole that is an example of nature at its most majestic and powerful. This is an empty land too. The weather can be harsh and the rocky, boggy ground is not that productive for farming, so although people live here and have done for thousands of years, their numbers are not high. With no big cities or even large towns, the natural world is dominant, unlike in much of Britain.

The landscape has been formed by ice and fire in the form of glaciers and volcanoes, along with unbelievably powerful earth movements that over tens of millions of years have squeezed and pummelled the rocks. It is impossible to walk here without noticing the skeleton of the land, the protruding bones that lie hidden beneath the surface in softer, earthier places. In many of the walks I have briefly discussed the geology behind the scenery, as I believe that a little understanding of how the landscape was formed (and I profess to no more) adds greatly to one's appreciation of it (see page 16 for more on the geology). The skin that covers the rocks is interesting too. Now mostly bogland, much was once woodland; remnants of this remain and, with help, it is returning in places. The fauna and flora that live in this austere land are touched on too, for again knowledge of these increases and deepens enjoyment.

There is huge variety in the North-west Highlands. One constant is the hugely indented coastline with many long fjord-like sea lochs running deep into the land. In the southern part of the area are the rough hills of Ardgour, Moidart and Knoydart, tangled together and packed tightly above narrow glens. North of these the hills straighten out, forming long ridges above longer, broader glens – Glen Shiel, Glen Affric, Glen Cannich, Strathfarrar, Strathconon and Glen Carron. Long

View north to Quinag from the Bealach Mor, Suilven.

lochs lie in these glens, many dammed and converted to reservoirs for hydroelectric power. North of Glen Carron the landscape changes and becomes wilder and stranger. The hills stand independent and alone, unusual shapes rising from low, boggy, lochan-dotted moors. As you travel north the spaces between the hills get bigger and the sense of vastness greater. The land feels stretched, pulled out by the tension in the rocks and the rivers. Then there are the Hebrides, only one of which, the incomparable Isle of Skye, is included in this book. Skye has all the glories of the mainland crammed into one small island.

The North-west Highlands are remote and rugged. Many places lie at the end of long, winding, single-track roads. Public transport is limited. Settlements are small and scattered, though the importance of the tourist trade means that accommodation, food and supplies aren't usually hard to find. Ullapool is the biggest town and a good base for the walks in the northern half of the area. For the southern half Fort William, just across the Great Glen, is the largest town.

The 24 walks in this book have been selected as the best, in the author's opinion, that cover the different landscapes of the area – hill, loch, forest, waterfall, coast. The highest hills, the famous Munros – mountains above 3,000 feet (914.4 metres) – haven't been included, as they are well covered elsewhere. The lower hills that are featured, however, are all as fine as, or finer than, any of the Munros and mostly far less frequented. These hills mainly fall into three categories – Corbetts (between 2,500 and 3,000 feet/762 and 914.4 metres), Grahams (between 2,000 and 2,500 feet/610 and 761 metres) and Marilyns (hills of any height with a re-ascent of at least 500 feet/150 metres on all sides).

Access

Scotland has some of the best access legislation in the world with a right of access to virtually all land. Of course walkers should treat the environment with respect and not do any damage (see page 13), and should also respect the homes and work of people who live in the area. The only access considerations for the walks in this book are the need to keep dogs under control during the lambing season, as there are sheep in many areas, and to take account of the stalking season, when deer are hunted, which lasts from 1 July to mid-October, though most estates don't start stalking until mid-August. When stalking is taking place, walkers should try to minimise disturbance to deer by following land managers' advice when available. Estates cannot restrict access to whole areas, however, or for long periods of time, and any notices stating such restrictions can be ignored. Estates may put up signs and noticeboards indicating where stalking is taking place. An increasing number take part in the Hillphones scheme, where you can ring up and hear a recorded message about stalking on an estate (www.snh.org.uk/hillphones/).

Weather

The best prediction that can be made about the weather in the Highlands is that it's unpredictable. The North-west Highlands have a reputation for being wet, as expressed in the old saying that 'If you can see Skye it's going to rain; if you can't see Skye it's raining.' Certainly geographical location, perched on the edge of the North Atlantic Ocean, puts the area in the direct line of storms sweeping in across the sea and gives it a damp maritime climate. Knoydart is the wettest place, with up to 220 inches (550 cm) of rain annually. On the other hand, coastal areas may have only 40–80 inches (100–120cm) of rain per year. Heading for the coast when the hills are shrouded in mist can be a good idea. From October to May the rain may fall as snow, especially on the hilltops and when the wind is from a northerly direction. However, the area rarely gets the heavy snowfalls found in the higher hills to the south and east. Temperatures are quite high for the latitude, due to the Gulf Stream. In summer when the sun is shining they can rise to well above 20°C, though around 15°C is more usual. Sunny weather can occur at any time but is more likely in May and June, when daylight hours are long, and least likely in midwinter. Below-zero temperatures are frequent in winter, especially high in the hills. The strongest winds occur during the winter too, though the area is windy all year round. The weather can change very quickly and waterproofs and warm clothing should always be carried.

Terrain and walking times

The terrain in the North-west Highlands is mostly very rugged with stones and bogs common. Oddly, the easiest going is often on the mountain summits and along coastal cliff tops, both of which can be grassy and surprisingly smooth. Because much of the area is relatively unfrequented, paths may be overgrown or indistinct and hard to follow. Many of the routes are cross-country and involve traversing rough and sometimes steep terrain. Times for the walks can vary enormously and much depends on the walker. A general guide for timings is Naismith's Rule, first worked out by the Scottish mountaineer W. W. Naismith way back in 1892, which allows for 3 miles (5 km) per hour and half an hour for every 1,000 feet (300 metres) of ascent, not including stops.

Safety

Walking in the North-west Highlands is generally a safe activity. However, many areas are remote and the terrain can be steep and rocky: people do get lost and have accidents. Leaving details of where you are going, and when you expect to return, with family, friends or at your accommodation is wise, especially if walking alone. Remember to let them know once the walk is over. If an accident does occur, the mountain rescue can be called by ringing 999 and asking for the police and then mountain rescue. As much information as possible about the location and the nature of the incident should be provided. Mountain rescue teams are made up of volunteers who give up their time to help those in need. They rely on voluntary donations and collecting boxes will be found in bars and cafés across the region.

A mobile phone can be useful in case of an accident, but note that a signal may be unobtainable in reémote areas. A phone is not a substitute for skill either, and walkers should be able to navigate and should carry the right equipment for the time of year and the nature of the walk. This includes footwear for rough terrain, warm and waterproof clothing, food and drink, first-aid kit, torch, whistle, compass and a plastic survival bag. Between October and May an ice-axe and crampons, and the ability to use them, may be needed on summit walks.

Long-distance walks

The walks in this book are all day walks but many can be linked to form longer walks. There are various other options for long-distance walks in the area too, including the Cape Wrath Trail, an 'unofficial' trail that runs from Fort William to Cape Wrath for a distance of around 200 miles (320 km). It has no set route, though the most popular ones are described in the two guidebooks to the trail. There are many options for variations, including climbing some summits. Other long-distance walks can easily be compiled by studying the maps.

Wild camping

All the walks in the book start and finish on roads, though several could be split over two days with a stay in the wilds. Wild camping (which means well away from roads and houses) is a legal right under the access legislation and a wonderful way to experience the North-west Highlands to the full. Nights out in wild places are a joy. Wild campers need to carry a tent, sleeping bag, stove and cooking gear, but none of these needs weigh very much; the load for a trip of one or two nights need weigh no more than 22–26 lb (10–12 kg).

Midges and ticks

Calm, humid days in summer, especially around dawn and dusk, can be plagued by swarms of midges, tiny flying insects with a nasty bite. Midges are less likely in heavy rain or hot sun and can't fly if it's windy. Choosing a breezy lunch spot is a good idea. Insect repellents are essential to stop them biting, though they still buzz maddeningly around your face. Some people like insect-mesh head nets too, especially when camping. Long-sleeved clothing is also useful, as midges can't bite through it. The most powerful repellents contain a chemical known as DEET, but some people react badly to this and it needs to be kept away from plastic items, such as watch straps, as it melts them. Although maybe not quite as effective, I prefer less harsh natural repellents such as Mosi-Guard Natural, made from eucalyptus.

Ticks are very tiny parasitic blood-sucking insects found in long vegetation such as grass and bracken. As you brush through these plants, ticks may attach themselves to your skin or clothing, crawl about looking for a soft spot, then embed their mouth parts in your flesh and swell up as they suck your blood. Checking for ticks at the end of a day's walk is a good idea. They roam around before biting so can often be located and removed before you are bitten. Embedded ticks need to be detached carefully, so nothing remains in the wound. A small pair of tweezers is useful for this and tick removal devices are available. Tucking trousers into socks, wearing a long-sleeved shirt and putting repellent on your ankles and any bare skin helps keep ticks away. If you do get bitten, keep a close eye on the wound after the tick has been removed and if it doesn't heal quickly, or if there is any sign of discoloration, swelling or a red mark, see a doctor as ticks can spread disease.

Leaving no trace

The environment in the North-west Highlands is quite resilient and unlikely to be seriously damaged by walkers. The real threats come from industrial developments, such as wind farms, pylons, dams, bulldozed roads and the like. However, bad practice by walkers can make places look tired and worn. A few basic good habits can minimise this. First, where there are paths try to stay on them, rather than walking along the edges, which can cause them to spread and become wide, eroded scars that look ugly and are unpleasant to walk on. In particular, don't cut corners on zig-zags on hillsides as the new paths formed quickly become run-off channels down which water runs, causing erosion. When walking cross-country, try to leave no

Slioch from the walk beside the Kinlochewe River.

sign of your passing other than footprints, which means not marking your route with cairns or any other signs unless you remove them afterwards.

All litter should be carried out, of course, including biodegradable items such as orange peel and banana skins, as these last a surprisingly long time.

If a toilet stop is necessary, choose a spot at least 200 yards away from paths and bury faeces in a shallow hole (a plastic garden trowel can be carried for this purpose). Toilet paper can be buried too or else packed in a sealed plastic bag. Only burn it if there is no fire risk.

A geological wonderland

The North-west Highlands is an area of major geological importance where breakthroughs in the understanding of how the landscape was formed were made. So significant is this area that the northern section, from Ullapool to Cape Wrath, became Scotland's first geo park in 2005. The North-west Geo Park is one of 35 such parks worldwide, all endorsed by UNESCO.

The main reason for the creation of the Geo Park is the Moine Thrust, a low-angle geological fault line running down the north-west of Scotland, all the way from the north coast to the Isle of Skye, mostly about 20 miles (32 km) in from the coast. The Moine Thrust marks the edge of the Caledonian mountain-building period some 400 million years ago. During this period Moine schists, the metamorphic rocks that make up the bulk of the Highlands and which were laid down as sedimentary rocks 800–1,000 million years ago, were pushed by incredible forces west-north-west over the rocks of the Northern Highlands. Along the line of the Thrust the geology is very complicated and confusing. West of the Thrust the base rocks are Lewisian gneiss, an ancient metamorphic rock, amongst the oldest on earth, dating back 3 billion years and named for the island of Lewis. Lewisian gneiss is very varied, often colourful and striped, as it is made up of many different types of rock – volcanic and sedimentary – that were buried deep in the earth due to tectonic plate movement and then changed by extreme heat and pressure. In places it is cut by intrusions of volcanic rocks such as granite. These are called dykes and form lines in the gneiss that add to the beauty and complexity.

On top of the gneiss in many places are sedimentary Torridonian sandstones, which were laid down around 1 billion years ago, and sedimentary Cambrian quartzite, which dates from around 500 million years ago. Both rocks form steep, dramatic mountains.

Lorgasdal Bay on the South Duirinish Coast.

A walker spans 500 million years with her hand on the Moine Thrust at Knockan Crag.

A puzzle along the Moine Thrust zone is that older Moine schists lie on top of these younger sedimentary rocks. Understanding how earth movements caused this by pushing the older rocks over the younger ones was a key to the development of modern geology.

There is also geological interest in the Skye mountains, which are the remnants of ancient volcanoes. Rock is so dominant in this area – much will be seen on every walk – that a basic understanding of the geology will greatly enhance appreciation of the region and enjoyment of the walks.

The National Trust for Scotland

The National Trust for Scotland is the largest conservation charity in Scotland. It is an independent organisation, not a government body, and so is reliant on donations, membership fees and grants. The NTS safeguards some of the most beautiful landscapes in Scotland, many of which are featured in this book, and works both to conserve and to restore them. It is a body well worth supporting.

THE WALKS

Garbh Bheinn of Ardgour

6 miles (9.5 km)

Although short, this is a strenuous walk as it climbs a high, rocky peak, whose name appropriately means 'rough mountain', and involves 3,117 feet (950 metres) of ascent. The rewards for the effort are fine rocky scenery and splendid views over sea lochs, islands and mountains. When snow lies this is a serious outing requiring good winter skills and equipment.

Garbh Bheinn of Ardgour (there are two other hills named Garbh Bheinn in the area) rises on the west side of Loch Linnhe, opposite the mouth of Loch Leven, and stands out as a big, black, ragged, dramatic rock pyramid from Glencoe village and the Ballachulish Bridge. It looks particularly spectacular at sunset, silhouetted against the darkening sky with flaming red clouds flaring around it. Garbh Bheinn is the highest and grandest hill on the big peninsula made up of the districts of Ardgour, Sunart, Morvern, Ardnamurchan and Moidart. This is the south-westernmost part of the Scottish mainland lying north of the Great Glen fault. The south-west part of the peninsula has an island feel, especially as the easiest way to reach it is by the Corran Ferry, across the arm of the sea called Loch Linnhe. The short sea crossing gives excellent views down Loch Linnhe to a scattering of islands, and many seabirds, including cormorants and divers, can be seen from the little car ferry.

From the east, Garbh Bheinn looks steep and intimidating, but the easiest ascent is no more than a steep, rough walk. This starts where the A861, which runs south-west from the Corran Ferry, crosses the Abhainn Coire an Iubhair. There is space to park near the attractive old stone bridge, which lies just upstream of the road. Buses operated by Shiel Buses run along the road from Fort William to Strontian.

Around 100 yards west of the bridge **1** a trace of a path heads up the long, broad, stony and easy-angled Sron a'Ghairbh Choire Bhig ridge, which makes up the western side of the corrie. The path winds up shallow gullies, over rock slabs and through broken rock outcrops to the 2,700-foot (823-metre) summit of the ridge **2**. The summit, marked by a cairn, affords a tremendous view **A** across the head of Coire Iubhair to the huge rocky east face of Garbh Bheinn and back east down to the dark slashes of Lochs Linnhe and Leven with the hills of Ballachulish and Glencoe rising above them. A short descent to the north-west leads to a col at 2,454 feet (748 metres) **3,** beyond which the rough path threads its way up steep, rocky slopes to the 2,902-foot (885-metre) summit of Garbh Bheinn, whose cairn is set right on the edge of the east face **B**. There is a dizzying view down into Coire an Iubhair.

It is possible to continue on down the north ridge, but this is steeper and rockier than the terrain so far and all but confident scramblers should return to the col between Garbh Bheinn and Sron a Ghairbh Choire Bhig **3,** from where a rough path descends through rock outcrops and boulders to the corrie floor **4**. A clearer path on the far (east) side of the stream leads down the corrie to the bridge.

From the corrie **C** Garbh Bheinn looks magnificent, a dark wedge of riven and shattered rock towering above. Ravens may be seen, wheeling and diving around the crags. This impressive rock scenery is built of gneiss (pronounced 'nice'), a hard metamorphic rock – which has been changed by immense heat and pressure inside the earth – made up of quartzite and feldspar. This gneiss has a beautiful striped appearance. It also makes for excellent rock climbing, as it forms big unbroken cliffs and is rough, with many hand and footholds. You may see climbers inching their way up the steep buttresses and ridges.

The walk back down the corrie is easy and pleasant, though the path is usually very wet and muddy, with the rushing, burbling, lively stream close by. Boulders and rock slabs erupt through the grass and heather everywhere, a reminder of the harshness that lies above. Coire an Iubhair means 'corrie of the yew trees', though none of those now remains.

A winter camp in Coire an Iubhair below Garbh Bheinn.

View south down Loch Linnhe from the Corran Ferry en route to Ardgour.

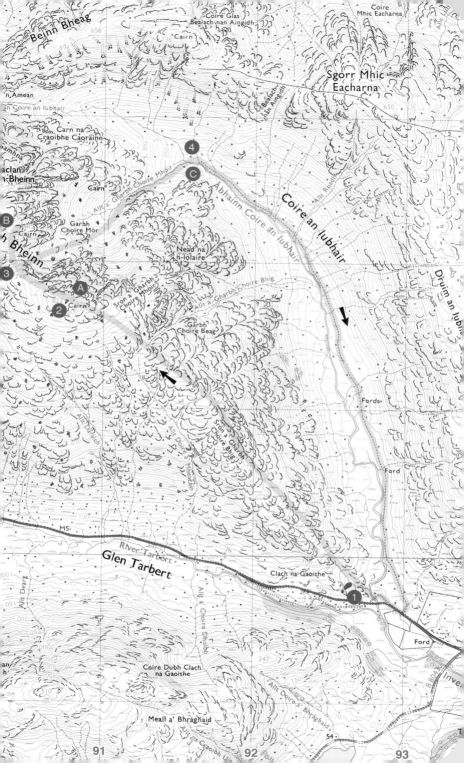

Loch Shiel and the Coire Ghiubhsachain Hills

10.5 miles (17 km)

Beautiful Loch Shiel runs south-west between the districts of Moidart and Ardgour. At 17.5 miles (28 km) it is the fourth longest loch in Scotland. There is much natural woodland along its shores, and steep craggy mountains around the northern end. At the head of the loch lies the little village of Glenfinnan. The Fort William to Mallaig road and railway run through Glenfinnan and there is a railway station here. The railway line crosses a magnificent, high, curving viaduct that will be familiar to Harry Potter fans as it features in the film *Harry Potter and the Chamber of Secrets*, with the steam train that runs along the line doing service as the Hogwarts Express. Loch Shiel itself features in the Harry Potter films as the lake outside Hogwarts.

Glenfinnan was famous long before the film-makers arrived, however, as it was here that Prince Charles Edward Stuart – Bonnie Prince Charlie – landed and raised his standard on 19 August 1745, beginning the last, ultimately futile, attempt by the Stuarts to regain the British throne. In 1815 the Glenfinnan Monument, a tall tower, was built to commemorate the clansmen who died in the Jacobite cause. The monument is now in the care of the National Trust for Scotland, which has a visitor centre nearby. The figure on the monument represents a clansman and not Bonnie Prince Charlie himself, as is often thought.

This walk takes in the south shore of Loch Shiel, two rocky peaks that are both classified as Corbetts, and some lovely natural woodland. It starts at Callop, 1.25 miles (2 km) east of the Glenfinnan Visitor Centre on the A830, where a turning leads across a bridge over the Callop River to a Forestry Commission car park and a sign announcing the Glenfinnan Native Woodlands Regeneration scheme. The restored forest here is made up of Scots pine with some sessile oak. From the car park take the forest track leading north-west through trees **1**, with the slow, deep, meandering Callop River on the right. After a mile (1.5 km) the track leaves the river and climbs over a rise before descending to the south shore of Loch Shiel **A**. To the north the Glenfinnan Monument can be seen, a thin pinnacle rising at the head of the loch, with the white houses of the village to its left. Follow the track out of the trees along the loch shore for 1.75 miles (2.75 km) to the old house at Geusachan **2**. Loch Shiel is long and narrow, with steep sides falling into the water all around and strips of forest along the lower slopes. Across the loch rises the massive bulk of Beinn Odhar (dun-coloured hill). Swans may be seen on the loch, while pied wagtails and common sandpipers dart along the stony shores. In early summer cuckoos call from the woods.

As you approach Geusachan, the pyramid of Sgurr Ghiubhsachain – peak of the little pinewood – dominates the view ahead. This 2,785-foot (849-metre) peak is the high point of the walk and is climbed by its north-north-east spur, which is rough and rocky with some optional scrambling. It looks harder than it is, two steep rocky sections being easily ascended via grassy rakes. The initial steep rocks can be bypassed by walking a few hundred yards up into Coire Ghiubhsachain from Geusachan then climbing west on to the ridge **3**. The lower part of the spur is heathery and grassy with some wet sections. Above 2,000 feet (600 metres) the ground is dry and mossy and the going easier. The first section of the ridge ends at 2,080-foot (634-metre) Meall a'Choire Chruinn **4**.

There is a short flat section beyond this minor top, then the final rise to the summit ridge and a short walk to the big, rather ramshackle cairn **B**, from where there are superb views right down Loch Shiel and across to long Beinn Odhar. To the east, knobbly Sgorr Craobh a'Chaorainn, our next destination, rises above the head of Coire Ghiubhsachain, with Ben Nevis visible far over its northern shoulder. To the south, Ardgour is a wild, rough tangle of hills.

From the summit **5** descend south-east, initially down steep grass and slabs. The going is easier than it looks and gentler terrain

Sgurr Ghiubhsachain from Sgorr Craobh a'Chaorainn.

is quickly reached. Pleasant walking leads round the head of Coire Ghiubhsachain with good views back to Sgurr Ghiubhsachain and ahead to the rocky knobble of 2,542-foot (775-metre) Sgorr Craobh a'Chaorainn (peak of the rowan tree). The direct ascent to the summit involves some scrambling, but the rocks can be avoided on the east side.

From the top **6** descend north-east over Meall na Cuartaige and down to the Allt na Cruaiche, where a path running from the Cona Glen to Callop is joined **7**. This path can be very wet and muddy but it does lead through some lovely old Scots pine and birch woods, part of which has been fenced to keep out deer and allow regeneration. There are good views to the north across forest to the Locheil hills. The stream widens to become the Callop River. The path passes the farm at Callop before reaching the car park.

View north down the glen of the Allt na Cruiache to the Locheil hills on the walk out from the Coire Ghiubhsachain hills.

The South Shore of Loch Hourn

13.5 miles (22 km)

This beautiful and wild walk fords some streams that can be difficult or even dangerous to cross when in spate, so it is best avoided after very heavy rain.

Loch Hourn is a wild, beautiful and remote fjord-like sea loch that forms the northern border of the equally wild, beautiful and remote peninsula of Knoydart. Loch Hourn means 'loch of hell', though today it is more likely to be seen as heavenly. Sailing it in a winter storm might give an inkling as to the origin of the name. Loch Hourn is long with a dog-leg in the middle. The lower loch is wide, the upper loch narrow and hemmed in by steep mountain slopes. The head of the loch forms another dog-leg and is even narrower. It is known as Loch Beag – 'little loch'.

This walk runs along the southern edge of Loch Beag and upper Loch Hourn to Barrisdale Bay, where the loch widens, then turns inland up Glen Barrisdale, before crossing a pass and descending back to Loch Hourn. The start at Kinloch Hourn is at the end of a 22-mile (35-km) winding, single-track road that runs from the A87 at Loch Garry far to the east. At Kinloch Hourn there are some houses, a farm, a tearoom, a few jetties and a couple of car parks. The situation is dramatic, with the glen and the head of the loch squeezed between steep, rugged hillsides. Follow the road down to the loch and along the south shore to its end, where the footpath to Barrisdale begins **1**. This is a good path and easy to follow, though it is often steep, muddy and rocky.

The path stays close to the loch for the first 1.25 miles (2 km) to Skiary, where there is a house and a small fenced larch and spruce wood. Past Skiary the path climbs a little, traversing steep slopes above the loch **2**. The path now undulates up and down, sometimes

close to the water, sometimes far above it, with a surprising amount of climbing for a coastal route. At times it is quite narrow. Mostly the slopes crossed are covered with a mix of grass, heather and bracken, but in places there are stands of trees, including Scots pine, birch, holly and rowan. The path passes above the buildings of Runival and the little island of Eilean Mhogh-sgeir, which houses a heronry **A**, and then the narrows of Caolas Mor. Throughout this section Loch Hourn is hemmed in by steep hills on all sides; it is only the smell of the sea, the seaweed on the shore, the rise and fall of the tide and the seabirds that remind you that this isn't a freshwater loch.

Beyond Caolas Mor the path climbs again and crosses a headland before descending to Barrisdale Bay, where a vehicle track runs south beside the loch shore **3**. Although Loch Hourn is much wider here, you still can't see the open sea. The Bay **B** is the delta of the River Barrisdale and is a lovely place, with a large expanse of stones and mud when the tide is out and steep craggy slopes on either side. Rising away to the north-west beyond the end of the loch are the hills of the Isle of Skye.

The track runs to the buildings of Barrisdale, where there is a stalker's cottage, a bothy, available to walkers for a small fee, and a campsite **C**. Accommodation can also be rented in advance in the stables next to the bothy and in a farmhouse – the White House – nearby. If you wish to finish the walk here, a boat ride across Loch Hourn to the village of Arnisdale on the north shore can be arranged.

Barrisdale is set in a flat area of marsh and wet meadow, with the eastern slopes of Ladhar Bheinn (hoof hill), a magnificent mountain, rising to the west and the northern slopes of Luinne Bheinn (swelling hill), another Munro, rising to the south. The track continues south to cross the Barrisdale River. Leave the track just before the bridge **4** and take the path running south and then east up Glen Barrisdale. This path is well made but is in poor condition and looks little used. There are remnants of forest – birch, rowan, holly, alder and a few pines – on the flanks of the narrow glen. Then 2.5 miles (4 km) from the bridge over the Barrisdale River the path climbs more steeply to where a stream rushes down from the north **5**. Looking up, a col can be seen high above. Climb the steep bog and grass slopes to this 1,640-foot (500-metre) col **6**, which lies between the two hills of Meall nan Eun (hill of the birds) and Sgurr Sgiath Airigh (peak of the shieling of the wing), either or both of which can be climbed from here if you want to bag a summit or two. There are superb views of Loch Hourn and Ladhar Bheinn from the summits. From the col descend through a lovely wood on the steep slopes beside the Allt a'Chamuis Bhain back to the path **7** beside Loch Hourn, between Runival and Skiary and so to Kinloch Hourn.

Walkers above Loch Hourn at Skiary heading west towards Barrisdale.

The Circuit of Beinn Fhada

17 miles (27 km)

Beinn Fhada is a mighty mountain, a massive hulking brute of a hill that stretches some 6 miles (10 km) from Morvich, just east of Loch Duich, to the head of Glen Affric. The name means 'long mountain' and is sometimes anglicised to Ben Attow. The top of the mountain is a big plateau sloping gently to the south, below which very steep slopes of scree and grass run down to Gleann Lichd and the Fionngleann. On the northern side, however, steep, rocky slopes fall abruptly into big corries, while the western end of the hill is a tangled mass of crags, buttresses and gullies.

Beinn Fhada is separated from neighbouring hills – A'Ghlas-bheinn to the north and Saileag to the south – by narrow, rugged passes. Paths and tracks encircle the mountain, and the circuit, which crosses both passes and visits the remote head of Glen Affric, is a superb venture into wild country. The whole of the walk takes place on the

The view up Gleann Choinneachain to the Bealach an Sgairne.

National Trust for Scotland's Kintail and Morvich estate and West Affric estate, and lies north-east of the famous Five Sisters of Kintail.

The walk starts and finishes at Morvich, where there is an unstaffed National Trust for Scotland Countryside Centre, the NTS Kintail Ranger Service, a Caravan Club site that takes tents and the NTS Kintail Outdoor Centre, which has a bunkhouse. There is basic accommodation along the route too, which may be welcome, as it is quite long. The Scottish Youth Hostels Association's remote and rustic Glen Affric Hostel (open April–October, no supplies) is situated at Alltbeithe in upper Glen Affric half a mile (1 km) from the route and there is a bothy called Camban **C** east of Beinn Fhada on the southern leg of the walk. Buses from Fort William to Skye pass along the A87 a mile (1.5 km) from Morvich. Cars can be parked at the Countryside Centre.

The walk is enjoyable in either direction, but I think anticlockwise is more dramatic so that is the route described here. Begin by following the road from the Countryside Centre to the Outdoor Centre **1**. A lovely strip of deciduous trees – birch, alder, ash, rowan, hawthorn – lines the River Croe and a footpath through these provides an alternative to the road for a short distance. In spring and early summer the woods are floored with flowers – bluebells, primroses, lesser celandine and more – which, combined with the fresh green of the tree foliage, provides a soft and gentle loveliness in stark contrast to the hard, craggy beauty of the hills above.

At the Outdoor Centre a signpost **2** points the way south-east down Gleann Lichd, a narrow, straight, U-shaped glen walled by the steep rocky slopes of the Five Sisters of Kintail to the south-west and the unbroken southern wall of Beinn Fhada to the north-east. A vehicle track runs 5 miles (8 km) down the glen to Glenlicht House, which Edinburgh University Mountaineering Club leases from the National Trust for Scotland. The walk along the track is easy, taking the walker deep into wild, spectacular country. To either side a series of streams rush down gullies, foaming white after rain, while the River Croe meanders along the glen floor.

A few hundred yards beyond Glenlicht House, the River Croe divides into the Allt an Lapain and the Allt Grannda. A path runs to footbridges over both streams. Once across the Allt Grannda **3**, the path begins a rising traverse across a steep hillside towards a narrow notch with seemingly no way through. Here the Allt Grannda is squeezed between steep rocky spurs running down from Beinn Fhada to the north and Saileag to the south **A**. The stream makes a right-angle turn in the constricted ravine and crashes down in a series of splendid cascades. Above the roaring water the path hugs the steep, rugged slopes before emerging into the more open upper Allt Grannda glen, where it fords many small side streams and continues above the stream until the latter turns abruptly to the south and into another gorge. The route now follows a subsidiary stream, the Allt a'Bhuic, to a gentle, almost unnoticeable, watershed at 1,115 feet (340 metres) below the little knoll of Cnoc Biodaig **B**. This is on the watershed of Scotland: streams to the east run to the North Sea and those to the west to the Irish Sea, though only a few hundred yards of almost level ground separates them.

From the watershed the path descends gradually to the Allt Camban and the Fionngleann (the fair glen). To the south rises a rocky peak called Ciste Dhubh (the black chest). The path stays above the boggy floor of the glen, passing little Camban bothy **C** before rounding the eastern end of Beinn Fhada and descending to a footbridge over the Allt Gleann Gniomhaidh at the head of Glen Affric, which stretches out to the east **D**. This is a wild, remote spot with big mountains all around. To the south, broad slopes rise to the long ridge of Mullach Fraoch-choire (summit of the corrie of heather).

To the north is the fine pointed peak of Sgurr nan Ceathreamhnan (peak of the quarters). About half a mile (1 km) to the east lies the Glen Affric Youth Hostel, one of the most isolated in the country.

Our route turns back west, however **4**, the path running alongside the Allt Beithe Garbh, which tumbles down from Sgurr nan Ceathreamhnan, for a few hundred yards and then traversing slopes on the north side of Gleann Gniomhaidh. After a mile (1.5 km) the path drops down to the glen floor and follows the meandering stream gradually uphill to the head of the glen. The path leaves the stream, which turns south here, and continues east to cross the watershed again – here another indistinct low rise just past the knoll called Cnoc na Cuaille **E**. Again the map shows no contour line between the streams running east and west.

At the watershed, big and lonely Loch a'Bhealaich appears; it is a desolate sheet of water brightened only by a thickly wooded island at the northern end of the loch – a great contrast to the bare, over-grazed ground round the loch. The path starts a gradual descent into wide, U-shaped Gleann Gaorsaic, another wild and remote glen, which runs north to the Falls of Glomach (see Walk 5) and Glen Elchaig. Our route lies westwards, however. At a path junction **5** take the left-hand branch, which runs to the foot of the loch and then traverses upwards across the stony northern slopes of Meall a'Bhealaich, an outlier of Beinn Fhada. The steep slopes of A'Ghlas-bheinn (the grey-green hill) close in from the north and the path passes through the narrow defile of the Bealach an Sgairne. At 1,673 feet (510 metres), the highest point on the walk, this is a dramatic pass known as the 'Gates of Affric' **F**. A'Ghlas-bheinn can be climbed from the pass and Beinn Fhada via a stalkers' path that starts a little way down the western side.

Below the pass Gleann Choinneachain runs through rocky slopes down to Dorusduain Wood, a conifer plantation dotted with the remnants of older mixed woodland, including some tall beech trees. The path descends from the pass by a series of zig-zags, then swings to the south-west away from the main glen to cross the Allt a'Choire Chaoil above a waterfall. It then descends to the Allt Choinneachain and follows this down the glen, with Dorusduain Wood on the right (north) and the steep rocky slopes of Sgurr a'Choire Ghairbh, another outlier of Beinn Fhada, to the south. The stream widens to become the Abhainn Chonaig as the view opens out to reveal the flats of Strath Croe and the waters of Loch Duich. Leaving the riverside, the path heads south across rough pasture past Innis a'Chrotha to a bridge over the River Croe **6** that leads to the road past the Outdoor Centre and back to the Countryside Centre.

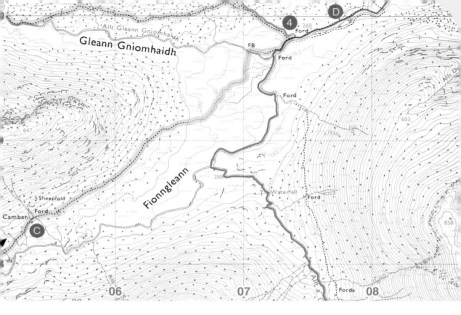

The dramatic narrow defile of the Bealach an Sgairne between the Munros of Beinn Fhada and A'Ghlas-bheinn is the highest point on the walk.

The Falls of Glomach

12 miles (19 km) via Carnan Cruithneachd
10.5 miles (17 km) via the Bealach na Sroine

High above Glen Elchaig, which runs east from Loch Long, the twisting ravine of the Allt a'Ghlomaich (stream of the chasm) comes to an abrupt end at the base of one of the highest and grandest waterfalls in Scotland, the mighty Falls of Glomach. These can be reached from Glen Elchaig by a rather precarious path that climbs high along the side of the gorge, but the most dramatic way to reach the falls is from above. The most scenic route is from Morvich at the head of Strath Croe (see Walk 4 for details of facilities at Morvich). This route leads up a wooded valley, crosses the remote pass Bealach na Sroine and descends to the top of the falls with excellent views of the surrounding rugged mountains throughout.

Return can be made over the little-visited hill of Carnan Cruithneachd, which gives a spectacular vista, though this does require fording the Allt na Laoidhre, which can be difficult when it is in spate. After or during heavy rain it is best to return via the outward route over the Bealach na Sroine.

The Falls of Glomach lie in a northern arm of the National Trust for Scotland's Kintail and Morvich estate. Most of the walk is not on NTS land, however. It starts at the Morvich Countryside Centre and follows the same route as Walk 4 for the half-mile (1 km) along the road beside the attractive wooded banks of the River Croe to the Kintail Outdoor Centre. Cross the bridge over the River Croe here **1** and follow a path north-east above the Abhainn Chonaig, through rough pasture and regenerating birch trees up Gleann Choinneachain (Walk 4 descends this path), with the dense conifers of Dorusduain Wood to the north spilling out of a big side glen up which the walk continues. About 2 miles (3 km) from the start of the walk, watch out for a faded signpost for the Falls of Glomach in the middle of a damp open area **2**. Leave the path up the glen here and follow the signed path to the fringe of woodland along the Abhainn Chonaig, where it drops down to a footbridge across which an open area in Dorusduain Wood is dotted with some big old trees – larch, Scots pine and Western Hemlock. To the east there are good views of the notch of the Bealach an Sgairne (see Walk 4), with the steep rocky slopes of A'Ghlas-bheinn and Beinn Fhada rising on either side **A**.

The awesome power of the Falls of Glomach.

There is no signpost in the open area across the bridge, but you should follow the path left to a forest road **3**. Turn right on this across the open area, past ruined Dorusduain cottage to a forest gate and into the trees and the Dorusduain glen, which runs north from Gleann Choinneachain. Take care to look out for signs to the Falls of Glomach at each track junction in the forest. Once in the forest turn left on the track **4** (ignore the branch running down to a bridge), which soon joins another. Now turn right **5**, heading north up the glen. At the next junction again keep right **6**, descend to a bridge over the stream and continue north on a track **7** through a cleared area to a final forest gate; here exit from the trees on to open hillside **8**.

A narrow footpath zig-zags up the steep hillside then makes a rising eastward traverse above the V-shaped glen of the Allt an Leoid Ghaineamhaich. The path crosses many small streams then, after 1.25 miles (2 km), curves north-east into a shallow U-shaped cleft leading up to the Bealach na Sroine at 1,706 feet (520 metres). The path traverses the hillside beyond the pass, then descends a broad rib between two streams into Gleann Gaorsaic just above the Falls of Glomach **B**. The thunder of the falls can be heard high above the glen, which is itself wide and placid, with the Abhainn Gaorsaic meandering through the boggy ground.

Above the falls an NTS sign warns 'Danger. Please take great care.' This should be especially heeded in rainy weather as the ground around the falls can be slippery. All that can be seen at first is the stream suddenly disappearing over an edge. Approach more closely and you can see the top of the falls. The deafening roar and sense of great depths just out of sight tell you that there is much more to experience. To view the falls in full, descend a steep path **9** down a series of grass and rock ledges on the left (west) side of the chasm. The falls slowly reveal themselves until, from the lowest platform, you can gaze down the tumbling water to a pool far below and look up to where it crashes over the lip of the glen **C**. The falls are in a narrow, cliff-edged ravine that echoes with the crash of the water. The effect is dizzying and the ground seems to shake under your feet. Initially the water falls free in a great white rush. Then, maybe a third of the way down, it spurts out of its narrow chasm, spreads out in a white fan, twists sideways, hits a great rock buttress and splits in two, rejoining just above the plunge pool – an exciting and awesome scene. Below the falls the Allt a'Ghlomaich runs down a narrow twisting gorge to the flat calmness of Glen Elchaig.

The Falls of Glomach are not just high but also powerful: they drain a large basin, the Abhainn Gaorsaic, running out of a chain of three upland lochs – Loch Thuill Easiach, Loch Gaorsaic and Loch a'Bhealaich – that lie between A'Ghlas-bheinn and Sgurr nan Ceathreamhnan. Sometimes they are said to be the highest falls in Scotland, but in fact Eas a'Chual Aluinn in Sutherland is higher (see Walk 17). Louis Stott, in his excellent *The Waterfalls of Scotland*, says 'clearly the height of the fall does not exceed 105 metres'. The exact height is immaterial: what matters is the sheer power of the water and the stirring setting – wild nature at its best.

The easiest way back is by the outward path. However, in clear weather a much more interesting route is to head west over Carnan Cruithneachd (wheat cairn), a splendid viewpoint, then descend south to Dorusduain Wood. The route is pathless until the hill has been crossed, so good navigation skills are required in misty weather. Start by climbing steeply south-west from Gleann Gaorsaic **10**. After 300 feet the hillside levels out and an undulating rising walk over an upland plateau westwards to the base of the final rocky pyramid of Carnan Cruithneachd ensues. Half a mile (1km) from the Falls of Glomach the Allt na Laoidhre is reached. Usually this stream is quite shallow and can be crossed on stones with your feet staying dry **11**. If it is in spate, however, head upstream, where it is often easier to cross. If no safe ford can be found, the outward path over the Bealach na Sroine lies just to the south and can be rejoined. Otherwise, once across the stream head directly for Carnan Cruithneachd.

The final climb to the little rocky summit is up grassy rakes and ledges, with some optional scrambling on little rock ribs and buttresses. The summit lies right on the edge of steep slopes above Glen Elchaig and the view along the glen is superb **D**. To the east, blue Loch na Leitreach fills the glen floor; to the north-west, Beinn Bhan of Applecross (see Walk 7) rises far beyond the foot of the glen. Westwards, a vast lake-dotted upland plateau lies to the north of the summit of Sgurr an Airgid, with the distant ragged silhouette of the Cuillin on the Isle of Skye (see Walk 22) on the horizon.

From the summit descend steeply westwards, picking a way through more steep, rocky terrain, and then cross easier, boggier ground to join a path running south to Dorusduain Wood **12**. After a short while the path becomes a rather crude bulldozed track leading to a forest gate **13**, through which a very steep track runs south through the trees to a much more easily graded forest road **14**. Turn left here and follow the road down in a series of long zig-zags, then continue beside the stream. The outward route is joined just below, where it crosses the stream **15**, and is then followed back to Morvich. In the clearing by the Dorusduain ruin, remember to turn off and descend to the bridge over the stream.

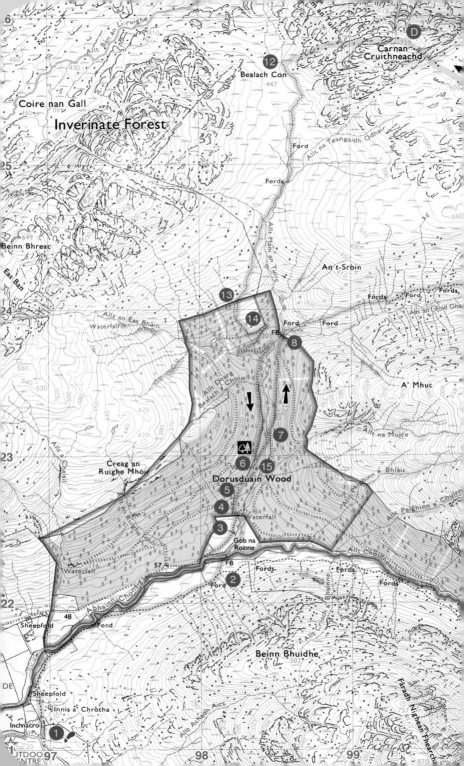

The River Croe meandering through lovely woodland at the start of the walk.

Around Loch Affric

11 miles (18 km)

Loch Affric is one of the most beautiful lochs in Scotland, a blue jewel
lying below big rolling mountains and with much remaining natural
pine and birch forest on its shores. This forest is being restored too,
mostly by the conservation group Trees for Life in conjunction with
the Forestry Commission, which owns much of the area. The nearest
town is Cannich, some 12.5 miles (20 km) to the north-east in Strath
Glass. There is a bus service from Inverness to Cannich but no public
transport down Glen Affric.

Glen Affric itself is a lovely wooded glen containing another fine
loch, Beinn a'Mheadhoin, and the third largest remaining natural pine
forest in Scotland. The importance of the native forest and the beauty
of the scenery are recognised in the glen's designations as a
Caledonian Forest Reserve, National Scenic Area and National Nature
Reserve. Film-makers have noticed the area too and the glen doubled
as the Canadian wilderness in a BBC version of *The Last of the
Mohicans*. A single-track road runs up the glen to a car park between
Lochs Beinn a'Mheadhoin and Affric. Lower down the glen it's worth
stopping at the Dog Falls car park and taking the short walk through
the forest to Dog Falls, where the River Affric plunges 10 metres down
a gorge: a 2-mile (3-km) round trip. There are viewpoints above and
below the falls, though from neither can it be seen completely.

The circuit of Loch Affric is a varied walk that goes from rich
woodlands to the open country at the head of the loch and back
again. There are splendid views of the hills on either side of the glen

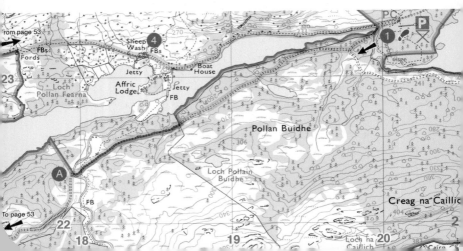

Beautiful pine and birch forests on the banks of Loch Affric with Sgurr na Lapaich rising in the distance.

and many fine trees, plus some regenerating Caledonian forest. The walk starts at the River Affric car park at the end of the public road, which is in a lovely setting amongst magnificent Scots pines, some of them over 300 years old, above the short section of river connecting Loch Affric with Loch Beinn a'Mheadhoin.

From the car park follow the track down to a bridge over the river **1** and then west along the south shore of Loch Affric. The loch is long, filling the glen, and at the eastern end very narrow, with the main section hidden by two promontories linked by a footbridge. The buildings of Glen Affric Lodge lie on the northern promontory. The track runs through woodland above the loch shore and crosses the Allt Garbh, which comes down from the hills to the south. Once over this stream the track runs further up the hillside and away from the loch **A**. There is much open ground here, and some superb views along the loch and across to the impressive line of big hills that form the north wall of Glen Affric. The two big dome-like hills north of the head of the loch are Mam Sodhail (hill of the barns) and Carn Eighe (file peak), which, at 3,874 and 3,881 feet (1,181 and 1,183 metres), are the highest peaks north of the Great Glen. Dominating the view, though, is the pointed and shapely peak of Sgurr na Lapaich (peak of the bogs) – in fact a subsidiary summit of Mam Sodhail – which rises directly from the north shore of the loch.

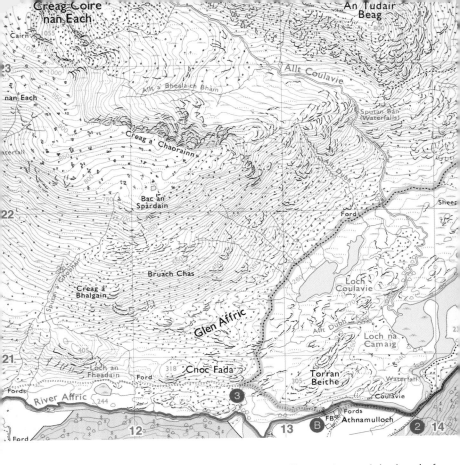

The track slowly descends to the River Affric just beyond the head of the loch. Stay with the riverside track at a fork **2** and follow it to the buildings at Athnamulloch and a footbridge over the river **B**. Just west of Athnamulloch is an enclosed wood. This is a restored forest. When the area was fenced in 1990 it was mostly bare, with just a few birch trees by the river. Trees for Life planted thousands of Scots pines here in the early 1990s and now it is a flourishing young forest with naturally regenerating birches, rowans and willow as well as the pines. There is rich undergrowth too, in contrast to the sparse, low vegetation outside the fence. Hopefully in the future the fences will be removed and grazing pressures in the rest of the area alleviated so the forest can spread.

South of Athnamulloch lies the huge corrie of Gleann na Ciche. There is more regenerating forest in Gleann na Ciche, where the Forestry Commission has felled non-native conifers planted decades ago and left them to rot, as taking them out would cause too much damage, and fenced large areas so the natural forest can regenerate.

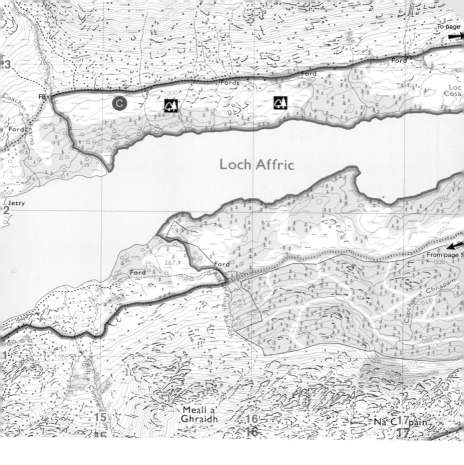

Ten peaks ring the corrie. These are often known as the Cluanie Horseshoe as they lie above Loch Cluanie and the A87 road and are most often climbed from that direction, though the Gleann na Ciche Horseshoe might be a better name. The great peaks of the horseshoe – Mullach Fraoch-choire (summit of the heathery corrie), A'Chralaig (the basket), Sgurr nan Conbhairean (peak of the keepers of the dogs), Sail Chaorainn (hill of the rowan) – are imposing when viewed from Athnamulloch and the path on the north-west side of Loch Affric.

From the footbridge follow the track 400 yards (0.5 km) up the glen to the base of the little knoll called Cnoc Fada, then leave it **3** for a footpath running north then north-east in a curve past little Loch Coulavie and around the base of the south-eastern spur of Mam Sodhail. The path, which is boggy in places, then traverses the slopes around 260 feet (80 metres) above Loch Affric, with good views in either direction **C**. The path descends to join a track at Affric Lodge **4** that runs beside the loch back to the start.

Beinn Bhan of Applecross

7.5 miles (12 km)

The great fish-tail-shaped wedge of the Applecross peninsula juts out from the mainland towards the Isle of Raasay, from which it is separated by the channel of the Inner Sound. To the south lie Loch Kishorn and Loch Carron, to the north Loch Torridon – long arms of the sea stretching far into the hills. The eastern side is bounded by Glen Shieldaig and the River Kishorn. The A896 runs along this breach in the hills. Rising above the road is a stupendous mountain wall of terraced cliffs and buttresses that curves round a series of six grand corries. This is Beinn Bhan (white hill), 2,939 feet (896 metres), one of the most impressive mountains in the North-west Highlands with some of the finest views. Beinn Bhan is a big mountain, curving north-west some 7.5 miles (12 km) from its foot at the head of Loch Kishorn. The long summit ridge is flat, with easy walking, but the slopes either side are steep and craggy. Beinn Bhan is formed of Torridonian sandstone, an ancient reddish-coloured rock that forms magnificent tiered cliffs.

The eastern corries are the finest aspect of Beinn Bhan and worth close inspection. This walk climbs into the corries then ascends the mountain by a spur north of the summit, returning along the summit ridge and down the steep, unbroken, mostly vegetated south-east slope. It begins at the bridge over the River Kishorn just west of Tornapress on the A896, where there is space for parking **1**. Oystercatchers can usually been heard and seen in the wet pastures here. A path runs northwards from the bridge, crossing streams running out of the southernmost corries. After 1.5 miles (2.5 km) the path crosses the streams running out of Coire na Poite (corrie of the cauldron). Leave the path here **2** and climb the rough hillside north-westwards to Lochan Coire na Poite at the mouth of the corrie. As you ascend through the heather, the cliffs and corries of Beinn Bhan unfold before you – a wonderful sight **A**. Two great rock buttresses – A'Chioch and A'Poite (the breast and the cauldron) – form the sides of Coire na Poite. The summit of Beinn Bhan lies at the top of the back wall. Good scramblers with a head for heights can clamber up A'Chioch to the summit ridge. Most walkers, however, will opt for the easier route up Sron Coir' an Fhamair (nose of the giant's corrie), the buttress on the far side of Coir' an Fhamair, the next corrie to the north. To reach this spur, head north-west from Lochan Coire na Poite across the mouth of

Coir' an Fhamair **3**. Sron Coir' an Fhamair looks a little intimidating, but the walk up it, although steep, isn't difficult.

Once on the summit ridge **4** it's an easy though dramatic walk round the rim of Coir' an Fhamair to the trig. point on the summit of Beinn Bhan **B**. The views down the shattered stratified cliffs into Coir' an Fhamair and Coire na Poite are sensational – a huge contrast to the calm gentleness of the grassy summit ridge. There are little lochans on the ridge and mats of dwarf juniper, as well as wildlife. I have seen mountain hares, ptarmigan and snow buntings here. The view from the summit is superb and vast.

To the north-east the Torridon giants Beinn Alligin and Liathach, steep sandstone terraced mountains with curving ridges, look magnificent. Far beyond them rises the jagged ridge of An Teallach, another monumental sandstone mountain. To the west the peaks of the Coulin Forest look big and bulky, while further away to the south-west Mam Sodhail and Carn Eigh above Glen Affric are a pair of clearly identifiable domes. South-east a jumble of peaks surrounds The Saddle above Glen Shiel.

However, it is west to the sea that the finest views lie: a tangle of water, islands and hills. The spiky Cuillin ridge on the Isle of Skye looks surprisingly close (it is 25 miles/40 km away), with the long undulating Trotternish ridge to its north. South of Skye, the equally spiky peaks

Looking up Allt Coire na Poite to the great buttress of A'Chioch on Beinn Bhan.

of the island of Rum can be seen. And far out over the sea to the west the dark hills of Harris in the Outer Hebrides, some 53 miles (85 km) away, lie on the horizon. Turning through the view, it changes from a mass of dark, grey-blue sea channels threaded between blocks

of land in the west to a complex, almost abstract, mass of shapes and colours to the east.

Only to the south is there a close hill, Sgurr a'Chaorachain (peak of the torrent), which is a smaller version of Beinn Bhan with an east face of corries, sandstone cliffs and buttresses. The most prominent of the latter is another fine rock spur also called A'Chioch. Between the two hills lies deep Coire nan Arr, with a loch on its floor. At the head of this corrie the Bealach an Arr links Beinn Bhan and Sgurr a'Chaorachin at a height of 1,870 feet (570 metres).

South of Sgurr a'Chaorachain a famous, or perhaps infamous, road crosses the mountains by way of the Bealach na Ba (pass of the cattle) to Applecross village. Originally constructed in 1822 and not paved until the 1950s, this single track road climbs steeply in a series of hairpin bends to a height of 2,050 feet (625 metres), making it one of the highest and most exciting roads in Britain. In winter it is often closed. The ascent of Sgurr a'Chaorachain from the Bealach na Ba is easy and short, if uninspiring until the summit is reached.

Keen walkers with plenty of stamina can cross the Bealach an Arr, climb Sgurr a'Chaorachain and then descend steeply into Coire a'Chaorachain from its north-east corner, go on down to Coire nan Arr and a walk out to the road. Most walkers, however, once they can tear themselves from the view from the summit, will be content with the descent of the south-east ridge of Beinn Bhan over some minor tops and then broad open slopes **5** back to the Kishorn bridge.

Through the Coulin Forest: Achnashellach to Torridon

10 miles (16 km)

Between Glen Carron and Glen Torridon there lies a wonderful and complex tangle of peaks, passes, corries, glens and lochans in an area called the Coulin Forest. A network of excellent stalkers' paths threads a way through this landscape. The crossing from Achnashellach in Glen Carron to Upper Loch Torridon takes you through wild and exciting country and over three high passes. There is public transport at either end – trains between Achnasheen and Achnashellach and post-buses between Achnasheen and Torridon village.

Glen Carron marks an abrupt change in the mountain landscape – a change due to the underlying geology. South-east of the glen the hills are green and rolling, with long ridges and few cliffs. North-west

The great peaks of the Coulin Forest seen from the hills to the south.

of the glen the hills are more rugged and rocky, with many cliffs and rocky outcrops and they rise up abruptly from corrie and glen floors. This is due to the Moine Thrust, a major low-angle geological fault line running down the north-west of Scotland from the north coast to the Isle of Skye (see Introduction, pages 16–17). The effect of the Moine Thrust is a huge difference in the landscape, as can be seen on this walk by looking back at the hills south of Glen Carron and comparing them with the Coulin and Torridon hills.

The walk is best undertaken south to north as the finest views are those of the Torridon mountains from the south. It starts at Achnashellach (field of the willows), where there are no facilities, indeed few buildings at all, other than the station. The area is forested, with many rhododendrons, and the start of the walk has an enclosed feel. A private road leads from the A890 in Glen Carron a few hundred yards to the station **1**. Cross the railway line at the station and follow a path a few hundred yards through big rhododendron bushes to a

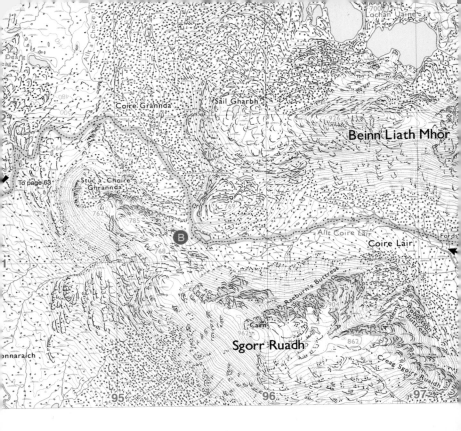

junction of forest roads **2**. Turn left here and go another few hundred yards to where a path cuts off left **3**. This leads through the trees to a gate in a deer fence and a path heading uphill beside the River Lair, which here runs in a narrow gorge. The path soon leaves the pine forest and starts to climb more steeply. Dominating the view to the west are the towering sandstone buttresses of Fuar Tholl (cold hole), an imposing fortress-like mountain. After half a mile (1 km) the gradient eases as the path enters long, curving Coire Lair **A**, a splendidly wild and magnificent corrie running between grand rocky peaks. On the right (east) side lie the long grey quartzite screes of Beinn Liath Mhor (big grey hill), on the left (west) the reddish Torridonian sandstone cliffs and buttresses of Sgorr Ruadh (red peak).

The path passes Loch Coire Lair and ascends **B** to the Bealach Coire Lair at 2,132 feet (650 metres), a narrow pass squeezed between steep spurs running down from Sgorr Ruadh and Beinn Liath Mhor, then descends 300 feet into little Coire Grannda. Turning west, the path now contours 400 yards (0.5 km) across the northern slopes of Sgorr Ruadh to the Bealach Ban at 1,804 feet (550 metres) in the

midst of complex rocky topography. To avoid Meall Dearg, a minor summit to the north, the path now descends slowly south-west across the headwall of Coire Fionnaraich and towards the big craggy dome of Maol Chean-dearg (bald red head) to meet a path climbing up the left (west) side of the corrie. Turn right on this path **4**, which runs from Coulags in Glen Carron to Torridon, and follow it up to the third pass, Bealach nan Lice at 1,378 feet (420 metres) **C**.

Below the Bealach nan Lice to the north-west lies Loch an Eion, a circular loch nestling in a curve of Maol Chean-dearg. The path descends to the east side of the loch, then follows the shore north-west to a junction with a path running round the west side of Maol Chean-dearg **5**. Loch an Eion **D** is in a splendid situation, with Maol Chean-dearg rising directly above. To the north the top of the long jagged ridge of Liathach, Torridon's finest mountain, can be seen, while far below to the north-west lies Torridon village. At the path junction turn right (north) and follow the path between little Lochain Domhain and Loch an Uillt'bheithe, then on a descending traverse across the eastern and northern slopes of Beinn na h-Eaglaise (mountain of the church) to the little village of Annat on the south-east corner of Upper Loch Torridon **E**. During the descent there are superb views across the beautiful loch to Beinn Alligin (jewel mountain) and across Glen Torridon to the towering ramparts of Liathach.

Coire Mhic Fhearchair of Beinn Eighe

9.5 miles (15 km)

Glen Torridon is one of the most spectacular glens in Scotland with two of the most impressive mountains, Liathach and Beinn Eighe, forming its north wall. The glen stretches 10.5 miles (17 km) from Kinlochewe south-west to Upper Loch Torridon, passing lovely Loch Clair, the classic viewpoint for Liathach, en route. The National Trust for Scotland has the Torridon estate in its care. It includes the whole of Liathach and Beinn Alligin, the third of Torridon's great mountain triptych, plus the very western end of Beinn Eighe. This walk is mostly on NTS land and runs up the long Coire Dubh (black corrie) glen between Beinn Eighe and Liathach, then rounds the westernmost peak of Beinn Eighe to climb into a spectacular corrie, Coire Mhic Fhearchair (corrie of Farquhar's son). There is a good path the whole way. Return is by the same route.

Liathach and Beinn Eighe are mountain massifs rather than individual peaks, each having several summits. Liathach is the most impressive of the two, as seen from Glen Torridon, with a succession of buttresses and cliffs rising straight up from the glen floor below a pinnacled ridge. Beinn Eighe presents a long, uniform slope to the glen that is uninteresting by comparison. The north side of Beinn Eighe is completely different, however: a series of huge corries divided by long rocky spurs. The mountains are formed of different rocks too. Liathach is mostly Torridonian sandstone, a dark, reddish rock that forms great terraced cliffs and buttresses. Beinn Eighe is mainly Cambrian quartzite, a hard, angular rock that is pale in colour and forms long scree slopes. However Liathach's four highest summits are capped with white quartzite, making the mountain very distinctive from afar. Especially distinctive is the quartzite cone of the highest summit, Spidean a'Choire Leith (peak of the grey corrie).

Liathach itself means 'the grey one', a reference to the quartzite caps. Liathach stretches 5.5 miles (9 km) from Coire Dubh west to Coire Mhic Nobuil and has seven summits. It is very steep on all sides and the summit ridge is narrow and rocky with many towers and pinnacles. Beinn Eighe is also 5.5 miles (9 km) long, reaching from Coire Dubh almost to Kinlochewe. There are eight summits, the highest of which, Ruadh-stac Mor (big red stack), is on a subsidiary spur of the main ridge. Although narrow and rocky, with pinnacles in places, the ridge also has broad grassy swards. Beinn Eighe is overall not as steep as Liathach and covers a much bigger area. Most of it forms part of the Beinn Eighe National Nature Reserve (see Walk 10). The name means 'file mountain', presumably a reference to the notched crest of the Bodaich Dubh or Black Carls at the eastern end of the mountain which can be clearly seen from Kinlochewe.

The walk starts in Glen Torridon at the bridge over the Allt Coire an Anmoich, near which there is a car park **1**. A signpost indicates the way to Coire Mhic Fhearchair and Coire Mhic Nobuil, pointing along a well-made footpath that climbs steadily north-westwards into Coire Dubh below the massive buttresses of Stuc a'Choire Dhuibh Bhig (peak of the little black corrie), the easternmost peak of Liathach, before crossing the Allt Choire Dhuibh Mhoir via stepping stones at the narrowest point of the corrie, where the slopes of Liathach and Beinn Eighe are less than 400 yards (0.5 km) apart. Ahead rise the sandstone buttresses of the splendid Beinn Dearg (red mountain), in the heart of the Torridon mountains, away from roads. Beyond the crossing the terrain starts to open out, with views to the north and west. The path curves along the slopes of Sail Mhor (big heel), the westernmost summit of Beinn Eighe, and the northern side of Liathach comes into view, even steeper and rockier than the south side with more and bigger cliffs – a truly dramatic sight.

About half a mile (1 km) from the stepping stones small lochans appear and a big cairn marks the path junction **2**. Take the right fork here. (The left branch runs west to Coire Nobuil and descends to Upper Loch Torridon at the west end of Liathach, another fine walk.) Our route heads north across sandstone pavements and contours round the end of Sail Mhor, which rises up as a steep buttress to the right. To the north-west is an unusual and extensive flat area of rock and water, a plateau of boulders and heather laced by streams and little lochans. Beyond this wild country rise the peaks of the Flowerdale Forest, pointed Beinn an Eoin and the bulky buttresses of Beinn a'Chearcaill (see Walk 11). As you round Sail Mhor a tapering ridge with steep scree slopes on its sides comes into view. This is Ruadh-stac Mor, the summit of Beinn Eighe. The stream running out of Coire Mhic Fhearchair appears, falling in cascades from the corrie lip, and the path runs above this, still hugging the slopes of Sail Mhor.

Abruptly, the path reaches the flat sandstone terraces at the mouth of the corrie and the splendour of perhaps the most impressive corrie in Scotland lies before you **A**. Just in front a big lochan fills the corrie floor. Beyond it rises a huge cliff, the Triple Buttress of Beinn Eighe. Deep gullies separate the conical buttresses. The lower sections of the buttresses are Torridonian sandstone, the upper sections pale, sparkling Cambrian quartzite. The rock strata slant, so the sandstone makes up a third of the East Buttress and half of the West Buttress. Below the Triple Buttress cones of scree run down to an area of pools and boulders. Cross the outlet stream **3** and walk round the lochan on its east side for the best views of the Triple Buttress and the great cliffs of the east face of Sail Mhor **B**.

A rough path runs up the corrie east of the loch to the foot of the slope leading up to the col between Ruadh-stac Mor and the main Beinn Eighe ridge. A steep climb up loose slopes leads to this col and an easy walk along the stony ridge to Ruadh-stac Mor.

Most walkers, though, will be content with reaching Coire Mhic Fhearchair and walking along the loch edge or sitting on the sandstone slabs contemplating the great cliffs. Once satisfied, turn and follow the path back down and round to Glen Torridon.

Camping in Coire Mhic Fhearchair below the great cliffs of Sail Mhor.

The Mountain Trail and Meall a'Ghiubhais

6 miles (10 km)

Way back in 1951 the first National Nature Reserve in Britain was created on the north side of Beinn Eighe, in order to protect and manage a tiny scrap of Caledonian pine forest called Coille na Glas-leitir (wood of the grey slope), in which some of the pines were 350 years old. The creation of the reserve is seen as the official start of nature conservation in Britain. Today the Beinn Eighe National Nature Reserve, now owned and managed by Scottish Natural Heritage, is magnificent and the forest is flourishing and expanding for the first time in over 200 years.

The reserve lies on the south shore of Loch Maree near its south-east end. Loch Maree is a big beautiful loch, 12.5 miles (20 km) long and up to 2.5 miles (4 km) in width, and the only big loch in the Northern Highlands not to have been affected by hydroelectric schemes. There are many densely wooded islands on Loch Maree. These woods are some of the most untouched and ancient native pinewoods left in Britain and the islands are also a National Nature Reserve. The loch is said to be named after St Maelrubha, who, in the 7th century, came to Scotland from Ireland to convert the natives to Christianity. Maelrubha was based in Applecross and established a church on Isle Maree (Eilean Ma-Ruibhe). However, the island was regarded as sacred and a place of supernatural power long before Maelrubha appeared. There was once a sacred tree here beside a sacred wishing-well. Pagan rites continued long after the arrival of Christianity too. As late as 1678 one Hector Mackenzie, along with his son and grandson, is said to have sacrificed a bull on the island to effect a cure for the gravely ill Christine Mackenzie. The men were censured for this pagan ritual by the local church, but the woman recovered.

The SNH Visitor Centre at Aultroy on the A832 between Kinlochewe and the start of the walk has much interesting information on the reserve.

The walk begins at an SNH car park beside Loch Maree, 2.5 miles (4 km) from Kinlochewe. A booklet on the Mountain Trail can be purchased from a machine here. SNH has constructed trails in the reserve so visitors can see the different ecosystems and the beauty of the landscape. The Mountain Trail is the longest of these, climbing

The northern slopes of Beinn Eighe seen from the Conservation Cairn.

high above the trees to give extensive views. The path is well made and well maintained, though still rough and steep in places, and makes a circuit through the reserve. Cairns mark the route, but it is still possible to go astray, especially where the path has been re-routed and where it climbs up natural stone steps and across rock slabs. Meall a'Ghiubhais (hill of the pine trees) has superb views and can be climbed easily from the high point on the trail where there is a cairn signed the Conservation Cairn.

As you would expect, there is much wildlife in the reserve. Woodland birds such as chaffinches, wrens, great tits, blue tits, great spotted woodpeckers and perhaps crossbills may be seen, while ptarmigan inhabit the hills and golden eagles and ravens soar high above. Red deer and mountain hares live up here too. Dippers can be seen by the streams at all levels. Pine martens, wildcats and foxes inhabit the forest, but are rarely seen.

The trail begins by passing under the road from the lochside car park **1** then climbing south through the forest beside the Allt na h-Airidhe. Where the stream turns to the west, the path leaves it and makes a traversing ascent across the steep hillside to another stream, the Alltan Mhic Eoghainn, and an attractive waterfall. The path crosses this stream and leaves the trees for open country. From here **A** there is a glorious view north over the trees and Loch Maree to the great buttressed south face of Slioch (the spear), a magnificent and interesting mountain. To the right of Slioch can be seen the straight, deep trench of Gleann Bianasdail (see Walk 12), a geological fault line. The upper ramparts of Slioch are Torridonian sandstone and have the distinctive terracing and steepness of such hills. However, it rests on a base of much older Lewisian gneiss, which has a silvery appearance and can be seen clearly below the dark sandstone. This is known as an unconformity, as there is a gap of hundreds of millions of years between the ages of the two rocks. Across Gleann Bianasdail the rocks are much disturbed and show the effects of powerful earth movements over millions of years. The escarpment above the glen on the western slopes of Beinn a'Mhuinidh is made of Cambrian rocks, mainly quartzite, which lie over older Torridonian sandstone. However, the top of Beinn a'Mhuinidh is Lewisian gneiss, far older than the sandstone or quartzite, which has been forced over the younger rocks by the Moine Thrust (see Introduction, pages 16–17).

Although the trees have been left behind there is still rich vegetation covering the ground – juniper, heather, bearberry, crowberry, sedges, mosses and more. This is much healthier vegetation than found in areas that are over-grazed. The rock here is quartzite and the pockmarks and white dots in it are the remains of the burrows of worms that lived over 500 million years ago, evidence of some of the oldest life forms found in Scotland. Due to the worm holes, this type of quartzite is known as Pipe Rock. The trail climbs steeply through the arctic tundra to the Conservation Cairn at 1,804 feet (550 metres) **B**. According to SNH, 31 summits over 3,000 feet (914.4 metres) high can be seen from here. Dominating the view though are Slioch and the dramatic rocky and complex north side of Beinn Eighe.

At the Conservation Cairn leave the path and head west across rough ground **2**, rounding little Loch Allt an Daraich, to the summit cone of Meall a'Ghiubhais, which can be easily climbed to the twin summits. The south-westerly one is the highest at 2,909 feet (887 metres) **C**. Beinn Eighe looks superb from here, as do Loch Maree and Slioch. Immediately south rises a spur of Beinn Eighe called Ruadh-stac Beag (little red stack) with huge 'boiler-plate' slabs on its north face. The summit of Meall a'Ghiubhais is Torridonian sandstone, which is older than the Cambrian rocks it rests on; this is because the Moine Thrust (see Introduction, pages 16–17) pushed the older rocks westwards so they rose up over the young rocks ahead of them.

The north-east face of Meall a'Ghiubhais is steep and craggy, so it is best to descend back to the Conservation Cairn and rejoin the Mountain Trail, which traverses north-westwards across a quartzite- and lochan-dotted plateau to a little lochan, named Lunar Loch by SNH to commemorate the first moon landing in 1969 **3**. Just beyond the lochan the trail crosses the An t-Allt and descends north above the

stream towards the deep, impressive, cliff-lined gorge of the Allt na h-Airidhe **D**. In the shelter of this damp ravine rowan and birch trees grow in great numbers. The bright green vegetation, a great contrast to the browner, duller hill plants, marks a geological change. The quartzite is gone, to be replaced by dolomitic shale, which is rich in lime and potassium, making for a much better soil for plant growth than the acidic soils common in the Northern Highlands. These brownish coloured rocks are known as the Fucoid Beds, as the fossils they contain were originally thought to be seaweeds (fucoids). In fact they are worm casts, the oldest fossils in northern Scotland. So rich is the rock that limekilns were built to turn it into fertiliser; they operated until the early 20th century.

The path along the top of the gorge is fenced for safety, which rather destroys the wild atmosphere. After the gorge the path leaves the burn and descends northwards back into Coille na Glas-leitir, where it joins the much shorter Woodland Trail **4** which leads back to the car park.

On the long rocky ridge of Baosbheinn.

Peaks of the Flowerdale Forest

15 miles (24 km) over Baosbheinn
12.5 miles (20 km) returning along Loch na h-Oidhche

The Flowerdale Forest, which sounds romantic and evocative though
not very Gaelic, is the name given to the area lying between the big
Torridon hills and Loch Maree. This is a wild area of rock, bog and
water, with a myriad pools and streams in between sandstone
pavements and tussocky bogs filled with cotton-grass and bog
asphodel. At its heart lies big Loch na h-Oidhche, which fills the gap
between the two long rocky ridges of Beinn an Eoin and Baosbheinn.
Both hills look impressive from the A832 between Loch Maree and
Gairloch. The circuit of the pair is a wonderful walk in remote, lonely
country, far less frequented than the Torridon hills. Hydroelectric
schemes have been proposed for this area on several occasions. So
far these have always been defeated, leaving this beautiful area wild
and unspoilt.

**The walk over both peaks is long and fairly arduous, especially in
bad weather. However, the walk can be made easier and a little
shorter by following the wide track alongside Loch an h-Oidhche
back to the start rather than climbing Baosbheinn.**

Baosbheinn and Beinn an Eoin are Torridonian sandstone and present
the typical steep terraced appearance of such rock. Baosbheinn is
particularly interesting: it is built of fragments of rock that fell from
crags and accumulated at the base of a snowdrift and marks the
approximate altitude of the snowline during the last Ice Age. This type
of ridge is known as a 'protalus rampart'.

The meaning of Baosbheinn is usually given as 'wizard's
mountain', from the Gaelic word 'baobh' meaning a witch, fury,
wizard or she-spirit. Loch na h-Oidhche below it is 'loch of night',
which could be connected. Beinn an Eoin is much less threatening,
being 'mountain of the bird'.

The walk starts at the Am Feur-loch on the A832 near to a large
green shed-like building. Cross the footbridge over the stream running
out of Am Feur-loch **1**. A lean-to beside the path contains information
on the Gairloch Estate Bad an Sgalaig Native Pinewood, which is a
new forest planted from locally collected seed of Scots pine, birch,
alder, holly, aspen, rowan and willow. You can see the young trees,

fenced in to keep out deer, during the first part of the walk. (Loch Bad an Sgalaig is a reservoir 400 yards/0.5 km west along the A832.) Walk past the loch, through the gate in the forest fence and head south-east along an estate track that runs through the new woodland between the two rocky ridges of Meall Lochan a'Chleirich and Meall a'Ghlas Leothaid. There are notices about the woodland and the area in places and a network of waymarked paths is being built. Keep to the wide main track, which has red waymarks, and ignore any junctions.

Reaching the Abhainn a'Garbh Choire, the track follows this rushing river. Just beyond a large boulder known as the Grouse Stone the track leaves the forest at another gate and continues across open boggy moorland to stepping stones over another stream, the Abhainn Loch na h-Oidhche **A**. The steep north end of Beinn an Eoin lies directly ahead. Leave the track 400 yards (0.5 km) beyond the Abhainn Loch na h-Oidhche **2** and head south-east to climb Beinn an Eoin, turning the crags on the left (east) side **3**. Once on the broad main ridge, easy walking over moss, grass and sandstone slabs leads over three minor tops to much steeper ground that rises to the short, narrow summit ridge. The rocks on this ridge can be easily scrambled over or else bypassed on the right (west) side and the 2,804-foot (855-metre) summit, which lies at the southern end of the hill. The whole ridge has superb views across Loch na h-Oidhche to Baosbheinn, which is seen as a whole range rather than a single peak, with four distinct tops. From the summit of Beinn an Eoin itself the Torridon peaks to the south look magnificent across a wild expanse of rocky ground dotted with shining lochans and silvery rivulets. Northwards, big, island-dotted Loch Maree looks lovely, while the massive bulk of Slioch towers above it. Further north a succession of hills ripples away to the distinctive spiky silhouette of An Teallach.

From the summit of Beinn an Eoin descend westwards **4** to the head of Loch na h-Oidhche **B**. The ground is steep, rough and rocky, but there are no difficulties as long as care is taken with route finding. A small locked bothy called Poca Buidhe stands beside the loch.

A tangle of little lochans lies south of Loch na h-Oidhche. Make your way through these south-westwards, towards the south-eastern end of Baosbheinn **5**. There is no path, but the going is easy over big flat sandstone slabs. Climb rough ground to Drochaid a'Ghorma Locha, the south-east ridge of Baosbheinn. A long, enjoyable 3-mile (5-km) ridge walk follows with splendid views throughout. The high point of Baosbheinn, 2,870-foot (875-metre) Sgorr Dubh (black peak) is halfway along the ridge **C**. The route zig-zags at first over two minor tops, climbs steeply to Sgorr Dubh, descends equally steeply, then runs in a straight line over three more tops to the final summit, Creag an Fhithich. There are some steep, tottering pinnacles on this last section which look dramatic but which can be easily bypassed.

The north side of Creag an Fhithich is too steep and rocky for a safe descent. However, the east slopes are less steep and a way can be made down these; backtrack slightly along the ridge to find the easiest route **6**. Once down the initial slopes and below the crags, descend north-north-east across rough terrain to the new forest and a bridge across the Abhainn a'Gharbh Choire **7**. From here a track leads north to join the outward track some 2 mile (3 km) from the start.

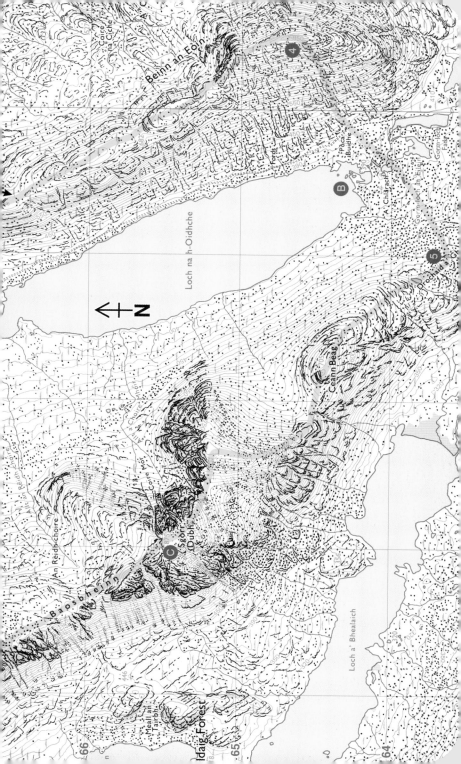

The Heights of Kinlochewe and Gleann Bianasdail

14 miles (22 km) over the Heights of Kinlochewe
12 miles (19 km) returning down Gleann Bianasdail

Kinlochewe is an attractive little village 1.5 miles (2.5 km) south-east of Loch Maree, at the junction of roads to Torridon, Gairloch and Achnasheen. It lies on the bus route from Inverness to Gairloch, Poolewe and Aultbea. The name is unusual as Kin means 'head of', yet Loch Ewe, an arm of the sea, lies over 12.5 miles (20 km) away, beyond Loch Maree. The answer to this puzzle is that Loch Maree was known as Loch Ewe until the 1700s, when the name was changed in memory of St Mealrubha (see Walk 10). The village is dominated by the pinnacled eastern end of Beinn Eighe, which rises to the west. To the north-west Slioch soars above Loch Maree, a great buttressed peak with a huge slash in the hillside below it called Gleann Bianasdail. This walk runs up Gleann Bianasdail to lonely Lochan Fada in the heart of wild remote mountains, then descends Gleann na Muice and the glen of the Abhainn Bruachaig, making a circuit of Beinn a'Mhuinidh, a huge plateau-topped hill north of Kinlochewe. This is an interesting geological area, as it lies on the Moine Thrust (see Introduction, pages 16–17). Slioch and Gleann Bianasdail can be seen well from the Mountain Trail and Meall a'Ghiubhais (see Walk 10).

The route crosses one potentially dangerous stream, the Abhainn an Fhasaigh, where it exits Lochan Fada (4) at the head of Gleann Bianasdail. Most of the time this can be crossed on large stepping stones. However, when in spate the water may sweep over these, making the crossing hazardous. Then it is best to retrace your steps back down Gleann Bianasdail.

The walk starts at a car park at the end of the minor road to Incheril half a mile (1 km) north-east of Kinlochewe, where a track heads north-west across grassy meadows and soon becomes a rough path **1**. The Kinlochewe River valley is flat and wide here and used as sheep pasture. Where the track reaches a gate don't go through it, but keep right on the less distinct path **2**. (The track through the gate leads to a burial ground.) There are lovely views across the Kinlochewe River to Meall a'Ghiubhais and Beinn Eighe as the path wanders along the

Waterfalls on the Abhainn an Fhasaigh in Gleann Bianasdail below Beinn a'Mhuinidh.

north side of the valley **A**. After half a mile (1 km) it runs next to the meandering Kinlochewe River, which has a fringe of oak and alder trees. To the right steep slopes rise to impressive crags above scattered birch woods. Slioch appears ahead, massive and bold, as the path leaves the river and reaches the end of Loch Maree, which stretches away into the distance **B**. In spring and summer the shores of the loch are bright with yellow gorse flowers.

The path now rounds the little bay of Camus an Trusdair, beyond which there is a headland containing the remnants of an old ironworks, one of several in the area dating back to the 17th century. Most of the extensive oak forest that used to line the northern shore of Loch Maree was cut down for use as fuel for smelting. The path curves inland across this headland to reach a bridge over the Abhainn an Fhasaigh, pouring out of Gleann Bianasdail, which lies dark, deep and craggy to the north.

Cross the footbridge and turn right along a path running above the stream **3**. For the next half-mile (1 km) the path is braided, with several branches running at different levels on the glen side. The best views of the stream, which tumbles down a rocky ravine in a series of lovely little waterfalls **C**, are from the lowest path, though care is needed when it's wet: the rocks can be slippery and in some places the path is on the edge of steep drops into the water. Just over 1.25 miles (2 km) from the bridge, the path starts to climb away from the gorge to round the top of a side ravine, reaching a height of 1,394 feet (425 metres). Looking back, there are superb views down the V-shaped gorge to Beinn Eighe. Ahead, wild mountain country opens up as the path traverses the eastern slopes of Slioch and descends to Lochan Fada **D**, beyond which rise some of the remotest mountains in Scotland – from left to right these are A'Mhaighdean (the maiden), Ruadh Stac Mor (big red stack), Beinn Tarsuinn (transverse hill) and Mullach Coire Mhic Fhearchair (summit of the corrie of Farquhar's son).

The path crosses the Abhainn an Fhasaigh on big stepping stones where it exits Lochan Fada **4**. Once across, faint paths follow the indented eastern end of Lochan Fada, a long loch that runs away to the north-west between steep mountain walls. Shingle beaches in the little bays are backed by grassy swards that make for easier walking than the tussocks and bogs covering most of the ground. In summer common sandpipers call from the loch shore and may be seen bobbing up and down on stones, while red-throated divers swim far out on the water, their high, eerie calls redolent of wild nature.

The sometimes indistinct path fords a little stream at the eastern corner of the loch **5**, then turns south and starts gently to descend

To page 83

From page 81

Gleann na Muice, here a broad, boggy glen with a chain of little lochs running down it. The path traverses across the northern slopes, just above the lochs and the glen floor. Once past Loch an Sgeireach and Loch Gleann na Muice the path enters a fenced area at a gate. A Letterewe Estate notice says that in 2004 this riparian area was planted with native species, including Caledonian pine from local seed, downy birch, sessile oak, rowan, alder, aspen and willow and that the deer-fencing is a short-term measure. Many young trees can be seen from the path through this large enclosure, which extends some 2.5 miles (4 km) to the Heights of Kinlochewe. As time goes on this will become woodland rather than moorland, a restored native forest.

The path becomes a wider track before you leave the enclosure and at the Heights of Kinlochewe, where there is a farm and some ruins, you join a vehicle track **6**. This runs down the glen of the Abhainn Bruachaig through sheep pasture back to the start of the walk. High on the south side of the glen is a long line of crags down which fall a series of long, thin waterfalls. These crags are the edge of the vast, little-visited boggy plateau of the Mointeach a'Bhreamanaich, which stretches away to the east. To the south-west Beinn Eighe comes into view again across the Kinlochewe valley.

From page 82

Fords

Loch Chùilean Dubha

Gleann na Muice

Abhainn Gleann na Muice

Ford

Airigh Shalach

Alltan Airigh Shalach

Kinlochewe
Forest

Ford

Ford

Doir' an
t-Seasgaich

Allt na Doire Bàine

Sròn Dubh

Loch an
Uillt ghiubhais

Doire Bhàn

Ford

Càrn an
Uillt Ghiuthais

Loch na
Guailne Idhire

Alltan Fearna

Fords

Càrn na
Seamraich

Garbh-Leathad

Sheepfold

Sheepfold

259

FB

Heights of
Kinlochewe

Ford

Allt Giubhais

Tòrr an
Fhithich

Waterfalls

Pit
(disused)

Fords

Ford

Waterfalls

Allt na Kinlochewe

Allen Cool a' Ghiubhais

Ford

Waterfalls

FB

Innis Dhrigeach

Waterfalls

page 81
Torran
nan Teud

Abhainn Bruachaig

Fords

Allt Dubh Leacaidh

Allt Dubh-Leacaidh

Waterfalls

Sheepfold

ochaid
hlinne

An Ochlas

05   06   07   08

Cul Mor and Knockan Crag

7 miles (11 km)

North of Ullapool, a little port town situated on Loch Broom and the best centre for walks in the far north-west, a line of strange and unusual mountains lies west of the A835. These are the hills of Coigach and Assynt – Ben Mor Coigach, Beinn an Eoin, Cul Beag, Stac Pollaidh, Cul Mor, Suilven and Canisp. Each peak stands alone and isolated from other hills, rising up steeply from the surrounding bog- and lochan-dotted low moorland like a fantastically shaped primeval giant. The low ground is made from Lewisian gneiss, an extremely old metamorphic rock that gives rise to poor soils and here creates the striking landscape of hummocks and pools known as 'cnoc and lochan' (from the Gaelic for knolls and lakes). The mountains are dark Torridonian sandstone, sometimes capped with quartzite, with the steep sides and terraced cliffs that go with such rock. This sandstone filled in the dips and hollows of the landscape below and in places you can see the shape of that landscape underneath, the undulating line of the Lewisian gneiss showing what it was like. East of the A835 the terrain is different with the more conventionally shaped hills forming long massifs linked with high cols.

The complex reasons for these topographical changes are explained in simple terms at Knockan Crag National Nature Reserve, run by Scottish Natural Heritage, which is on the A835 12.5 miles (20 km) north of Ullapool opposite Cul Mor. The unstaffed visitor centre here has interpretation and interactive displays, and there are three circular trails with rock art and fragments of poetry by Norman MacCaig, who was inspired by the landscape here. The whole area from Knockan Crag north to Cape Wrath was designated a European Geo Park in 2004 because of both its outstanding landscape and its international importance as the place where a breakthrough in geological understanding was made. This was that, over the millennia, violent earth movements could force rocks sideways, sometimes resulting in their being piled up on top of each other in non-chronological layers. The low-angle fault line resulting from such movements is called a thrust. This idea, which went against the prevailing geological wisdom, was confirmed in the 1880s and 1890s by the field research of two geologists, Benjamin Peach and John Horne; they are commemorated in a monument beside Loch Assynt, just to the north of Knockan Crag. Thrusts occur when two continents collide. The layers of rock at the edges of the continents are squeezed together until they start to break and are forced over each other, resulting in mountain ranges.

This happened here when ancient continents collided and the rocks were pushed up to form the Caledonian mountains, of which the Scottish Highlands are a remnant. This is the Moine Thrust (see Introduction, pages 16–17), which runs down the line of the A835 here. At Knockan Crag you can see clearly where it pushed older rocks over younger ones, as dark Moine schists around a billion years old lie on top of pale Cambrian limestone that is 500 million years old. You can actually bridge the 500-million-year gap with your hand.

The crag itself, which runs for a mile or so high above the road, derives its name from the Gaelic Creag a'Cnocain, which means 'crag of the small hill'. The longest circular trail at Knockan Crag, the Crag Top Trail, which crosses the Moine Thrust, can be walked in an hour and, combined with an ascent of Cul Mor, makes an excellent day out. There are superb views of Cul Mor and the other Coigach hills from the top of Knockan Crag, and excellent views of Knockan Crag from Cul Mor.

Cul Mor (big back) is the highest of the Coigach hills at 2,784 feet (849 metres) and has two distinct summits with a big curving saddle between them. The eastern slopes are relatively gentle as they run down to the bright greenness of Elphin, where limestone provides a rich soil. The other sides are much steeper and rockier, with many terraced sandstone cliffs. Since 2005 Cul Mor has been owned by the local community in the form of the Assynt Foundation, which is working with the John Muir Trust, which assisted with the purchase, on the conservation of the area.

The start of the ascent of Cul Mor is at a car park 300 yards north of the Knockan Crag Visitor Centre. From a gate in the car park a good path **1** heads north across rough pasture and on to typical rock, bog and pool (cnoc and lochan) Lewisian gneiss terrain above Lochan Fhionnlaidh. The path turns to the north-west and starts to climb the south-east shoulder of Cul Mor, fading away before the top, Meallan Diomhain, is reached **2**. Although most of Cul Mor is dark Torridonian sandstone, this ridge is a big finger of pale Cambrian quartzite. Continue to the summit of Meallan Diomhain, then turn north to a tiny lochan and the edge of the cliffs of the north face **3**.

A steep climb south-west along the edge of Coire Gorm leads to the summit of Cul Mor, which is made of quartzite **A**. There is a trig. point here. The view is superb, with the vast, strange, wild flatlands of stone and water stretching out to the distinctive isolated hills of

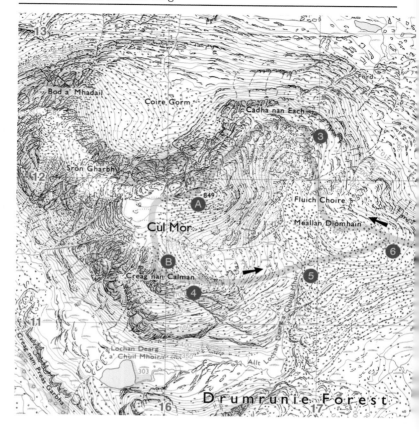

Suilven and Canisp to the north. Westwards is huge Loch Sionascaig, which has an incredibly convoluted shoreline and is dotted with islands. Beyond lies the sea at Elphan Bay. Southwards rises the weird pinnacled ridge of Stac Pollaidh, a rotting sandstone peak, though this is better seen from Creag nan Calman, the lower summit of Cul Mor.

From the summit head west, then south down to a broad col **4**. A short climb leads to the second top, 2,715-foot (828-metre) Creag nan Calman (crag of the dove), whose summit cairn is perched right on the edge of the steep west face **B**. A tiny cap of quartzite makes up its summit. Descend the east ridge of this peak **5** into a corrie and a complex area of boulders, hummocks, boggy ground and streams. Head slightly north of east across the corrie to avoid the chasm of the Allt Lochan Dearg a'Chuil Mhoir **6**, which slices through the hillside. Once across the stream continue east to the outward path **7** on the slopes of Meallan Diomhain and follow this back to the start.

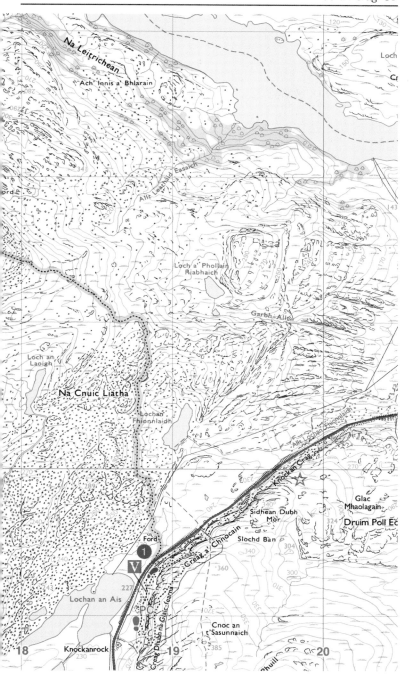

Cul Mor rising above the shining waters of Loch Veyatie.

Around the Cam Loch

8 miles (13 km)

As well as spectacular mountains, the district of Assynt has many large, beautiful lochs. The Cam Loch, lying just north of the crofting community of Elphin and the A835 road, is one of these. 'Cam' means 'crooked' or 'distorted' and presumably refers to the twisting shoreline with its many bays and promontories, features that, along with wonderful mountain views, make a circuit of the loch an interesting outing.

The scattered village of Elphin is set in green fields of a lushness unusual in the North-west Highlands. The reason is a band of limestone, which provides much richer soil than the usual Highland rock. There is an excellent teahouse in Elphin. In 2005 the Cam Loch was bought by the local community in the form of the Assynt Foundation as part of the Glencanisp estate – which also includes the mountains Suilven (see Walk 15) and Canisp – with the aim of conserving its natural beauty and restoring and expanding damaged and threatened habitats.

The Cam Loch trends south-east to north-west, the usual direction of lochs in this area and the direction in which the ice flowed during the last ice age. The loch lies on a geological fault line and was gouged out by ice and flood waters when the ice melted. The Moine Thrust (see Introduction, pages 16–17) passes across the foot of the loch, intersecting a small fault running at right angles to it. The rock at this end of the loch consists of short strips of pale quartzite and darker mudstone Fucoid Beds (see Walk 12). Either side of the middle section of the loch is quartzite, then at the upper end this changes to Lewisian gneiss. Bands of dark Torridonian sandstone reach down to the loch on either side, a narrow band separating two sections of gneiss on the north shore and a wider one between the gneiss and the quartzite on the south shore. On the circuit of the loch all these rocks can be seen easily and you often walk on them. It's interesting to try to work out just where you cross from one type to another and what difference they make to the landscape.

The circuit of the Cam Loch starts on the A835 400 yards (0.5 km) east of the bridge over the Ledmore River, where a signpost indicates 'Lochinver 12 miles' along a path heading north-west **1**. The loch can't be seen at this point. Set off on this path over a low knoll to a stunning view of Suilven (see Walk 15), which stands out beyond the end of the loch **A**, a distinctive hump-backed Torridonian sandstone hill with two steep peaks, one wedge-shaped, one a pyramid. The path leads down to a shingle beach at the narrow eastern end of the loch, then curves round to follow the north-east shore. After half a mile (1 km) it reaches a gate in a tall deer fence. Once through this, the footpath runs just above the water below the rough and craggy slopes of Creag na h-Innse Ruaidhe to Cul na h-Innse Ruadh, where a

small stream comes down a shallow valley to the north. There are little stands of birches and rowan, with the occasional willow, beside the loch and in spring and summer a scattering of woodland flowers – primrose, dog violet, lesser celandine. Chaffinches dart amongst the foliage, and in May and June cuckoos can be heard calling and occasionally seen flying hawk-like between trees. Out on the loch you may see ducks of various species and red- and black-throated divers. Across the loch Cul Mor (see Walk 13) looks superb, its symmetrical twin summits rising above steep craggy shoulders.

After the stream crossing the path divides **2**. The faint left-hand branch peters out after 400 yards (0.5 km); the right-hand one climbs round Creag a'Chaise, a little crag that falls steeply to the loch, then turns north along the Druim nan

The view along the Cam Loch to Suilven from near the start of the walk.

Cnaimhseag before continuing westwards to Lochinver. Where the path reaches the crest of this ridge, leave it and continue north-west above the loch **3**. There are traces of a path in places, but these are indistinct and fade away frequently so aren't worth trying to follow. The going over grass, heather, tussocks, flat rocks and bits of bog is not hard and with the loch to follow navigation is easy. In places you can walk on shingle beaches by the water. Throughout the walk along this side of the loch, Suilven draws the eye, gradually growing in size as you walk towards it. To the north rises Canisp, a great whaleback of a hill, higher than Suilven but not nearly so distinctive.

Looking over the Cam Loch to Cul Beag and Cul Mor. 'Cam', meaning 'crooked

At the head of the loch a slow, deep, meandering stream, the Allt na Braclaich, runs into the loch. To cross this go upstream to where it widens and becomes faster flowing and shallower, then you can cross on stones without getting your feet wet **4**. Depending on how much rain has fallen recently, this may be 200–400 yards (0.5 km) from the loch. Once across the stream, walk back to the loch, where there is a lovely sandy beach backed by a lush green sward with steep crags rising to the south – an idyllic setting for a rest **B**. To the east the loch stretches out amongst low hummocky knolls to distant hills; no high mountains break the horizon, which is unusual in this area.

To avoid the crags that fall to the water here, backtrack away from the loch a short distance then climb a steep slope to gain the top of the crags **5**. Staying well above the water, head south-west across more broken, hummocky ground. There are more big bays and promontories along the shore here than on the north side, but there is

torted', refers to the shape of the loch with its many bays and promontories.

no need to stay close to it. Indeed, the best views are from above the loch, looking across the blue water. There are more little patches of woodland in places, but for mountain views you have to turn back to Suilven or away from the loch to Cul Mor. As you approach the end of the loch the startling contrast between the bright greenness of the limestone scenery around Elphin and the duller, browner terrain around you is very noticeable.

When you reach the last promontory, Airdean Dubha, turn south **6** and head for a bridge **7** over the short, fast and deep river linking the Cam Loch with Loch Veyatie. Ironically, this very short stretch of water is called the Abhainn Mhor, which means 'big river'. It is a pretty stream, with little waterfalls cutting through slabs of quartzite. Across the bridge turn right and follow the river to the track **8** that leads from the fish hatchery on Loch Veyatie to the A835, then walk along the road for 1.25 miles (2 km) east to the start.

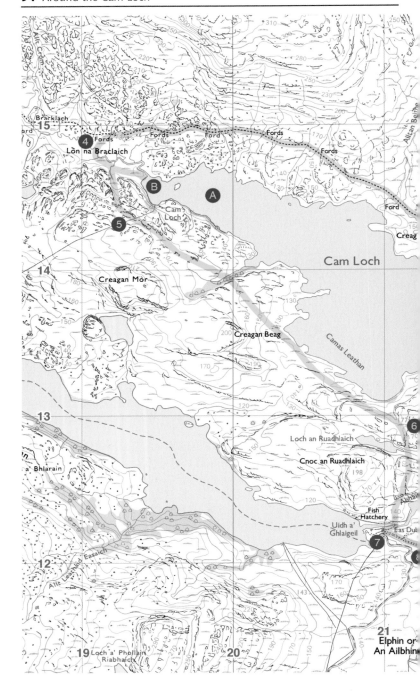

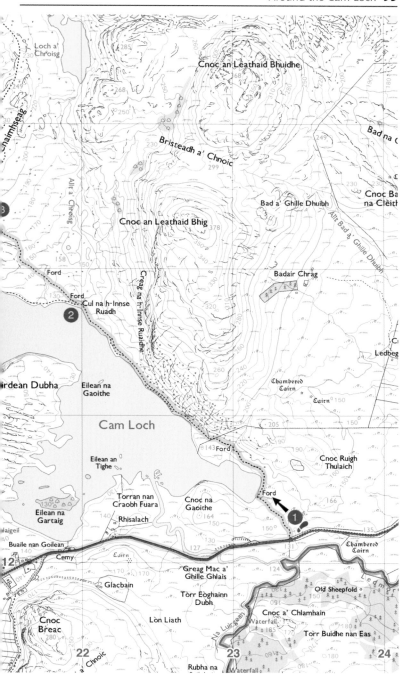

Suilven

16 miles (26 km)

Suilven is the iconic mountain of the far north-west, rising alone and dramatic from a flat expanse of bog and rock. End on, it is a spire from the east, a pyramid with curving sides from the west. From the sides it is a long, steep ridge with a low point just off-centre, a bulbous summit at one end and a pointed one at the other. From nowhere does it look less than imposing. Yet at 2,397 feet (731 metres) it is small on the scale of Scottish hills – nowhere near magic Munro status (3,000 feet/914.4 metres). If any hill shows that height is unimportant compared with appearance and situation, it's Suilven.

The mountain is formed of layers of dark Torridonian sandstone sitting on a platform of pale Lewisian gneiss and consists of a narrow, steep-sided ridge some 1.5 miles (2.5 km) long – a slice of rock

Looking south along the ridge of Suilven to Meall Meadhonach at the eastern end of the mountain. To the left Canisp rises above Loch na Gainimh.

towering above the flat lands round about. The name Suilven is Norse and means 'the pillar', which must refer to the west end of the hill, perhaps as seen from the sea.

Suilven is a remote hill, lying in the heart of a vast roadless area of bog, lochan and mountain between the coast and the A835, and all approaches are long. A superb circuit, described here, is to traverse the mountain, starting at Inverkirkaig and finishing at Lochinver further north on the coast. This walk is 12.5 miles (20 km) long if transport can be arranged from Lochinver back to the start. If not, there is a 3.5-mile (6-km) road walk between the two. The walking is mostly easy, on footpaths and tracks, the only steep slopes being on Suilven itself.

Lochinver is an attractive and interesting fishing port and the largest town on the western seaboard north of Ullapool. It has all facilities plus a superb view inland to Suilven and Canisp. The Visitor Centre has interesting displays about the area and the Assynt Crofters Trust. Also recommended are the delicious home-made pies at

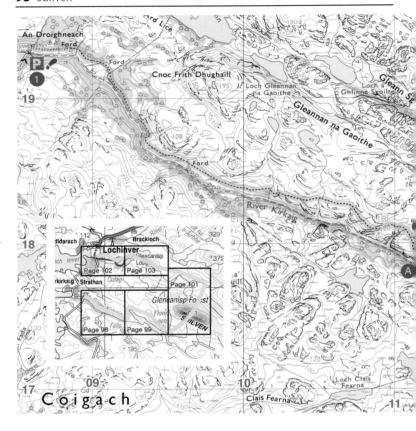

Lochinver Larder at the north end of the village. There are daily buses to Lochinver from Ullapool and Durness.

Inverkirkaig is a sprawling village spread out around the head of Loch Kirkaig south of Lochinver. The most attractive approach to Suilven starts half a mile (1 km) east of Inverkirkaig at the car park at Inverkirkaig Bridge, just below the excellent Achins tearoom, craft shop and bookshop – a remote situation for such an establishment. From here a signposted path **1** runs for 2 miles (3 km) above the narrow trench containing the lovely tree-lined River Kirkaig to the Falls of Kirkaig, mostly on open hillside above the river. Suilven is hidden from view during this initial stage of the walk. The path divides just before the falls **2**. To see them take the right branch, which is signposted for the falls and which descends steeply to some rock steps near the base of the falls. The Falls of Kirkaig **A** are near enough the perfect waterfall. The river falls some 60 feet (18 metres) straight down a cleft in sheer

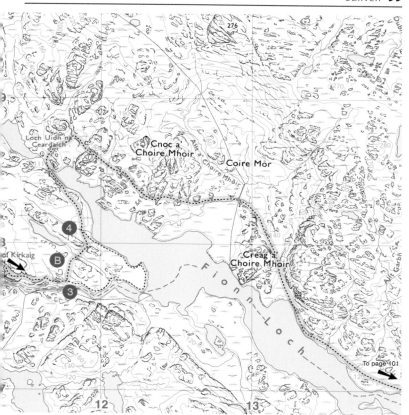

cliffs in a rush of surging white water to a deep pool. Trees grow right up to the rim of the falls, creating a lovely scene that combines natural beauty with awesome natural power. Fed by a succession of big lochs, the falls are always full. Salmon run up the River Kirkaig but are stopped by the falls and in season can be seen leaping in the pool below.

From the falls, return to the junction and continue on the path up the Kirkaig glen towards big Fionn Loch (fair loch). Suilven suddenly and magnificently comes into view as you approach the loch **B**. About 400 yards (0.5 km) before the loch a side path heads off to the left (north) **3** across boggy ground; this cuts off a long meander round the loch shore, so it's worth taking. It rejoins the main path after 400 yards (0.5 km) **4**. Continue on the path round the west end of Fionn Loch, then east above the loch to a stream running down from the low point on Suilven, which is called the Bealach Mor (big pass). The terrain is a mix of little rocky knolls and flat, heather-covered

The powerful Falls of Kirkaig pour down through a rock cleft between wooded buttresses.

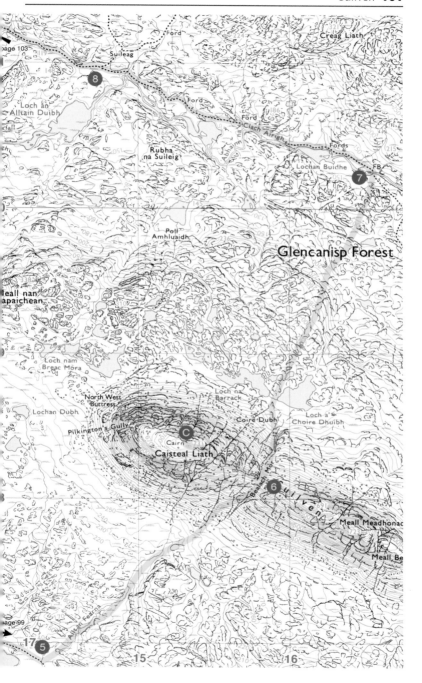

moorland. In places paths cut off to the north, towards Suilven. Ignore these and continue on to the stream, then turn up towards Suilven on a path, boggy at first, marked by a cairn **5**. The path climbs beside the stream, flattens out for a short while, then becomes much steeper and eroded as it climbs scree and heather above a gully before traversing upwards across the final slopes to the pass.

Turn left (north-west) at the pass for the short, steep walk, with a little easy scrambling, to the highest summit of Suilven, Caisteal Liath (grey castle), which is covered with turf. A surprise not far above the pass is a drystone wall crossing the ridge and dropping steeply on either side. Why or when this ridiculous wall was built no one seems to know. The view from the surprisingly spacious summit is magnificent **C**. Out to the west lie Lochinver and the island-dotted sea. On clear days the Western Isles are visible on the far horizon. There are also views of the surrounding mountains – Canisp and Cul Mor quite close by, Stac Pollaidh and Quinag further away, Foinaven and Arkle far to the north, Ben More Assynt and Conival away to the east, An Teallach to the south – and the gently undulating low plateau of rock, bog, loch and stream from which they rise. It's a wild, watery landscape, sparkling silver in sunlight, carved by the glaciers of the last ice age, as was Suilven as the ice ground past it on either flank.

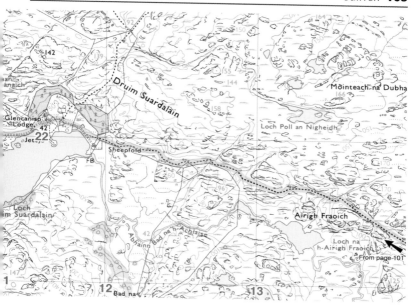

Walking back down to the pass the fine, steep-sided spire of the eastern tops – Meall Mheadhonach and Meall Bheag – soars ahead. The latter peak can be reached only by exposed scrambling and so is best left to those with the skills and the head for heights needed. There is also no safe way off Caisteal Liath other than to return to the Bealach Mor, from where you can descend the north side of Suilven by way of a loose shallow gully full of scree, rocks and heather. The very eroded top section can be avoided by a traversing path on the east side **6**. A rough path continues north over easier ground, passes between two lochans and joins the path from Elphin to Lochinver at a footbridge **7** over the Abhainn na Craich Airigh just east of Loch na Gainimh. Turn left (north-west) and follow this path as it weaves its way through the water and rock landscape above the river and a series of lochans. At a path junction **8** near Suileag bothy (a useful shelter in stormy weather) keep left. Eventually the path reaches gentler, softer terrain at Loch Druim Suardalain on the shores of which stands Glencanisp Lodge. Here the path becomes a track and, after another half-mile (1 km), a minor road that leads to a fine view over Lochinver harbour and then a descent into the town itself. Cars can be parked at the end of the minor road, so if you have two vehicles one could be left here and the other at the start at Inverkirkaig. If not, there remains the 3.5-mile (6-km) walk along the winding road back to the start.

Quinag

8 miles (13 km)

Quinag is one of the great mountains of north-west Scotland, a huge massif formed of curving ridges and soaring buttresses and with three main peaks. Quinag takes the form of a curved letter Y with three big arms radiating out to summits below which lie massive broken crags. Deep rocky corries lie between the arms and deep cols between the peaks. Quinag looks impressive from any direction, but particularly from around Kylesku to the north, from where the huge buttresses of the two northerly peaks, Sail Gharbh and Sail Gorm, sweep into the sky. On the west side a long line of cliffs runs the length of the mountain, which appears as a colossal unbroken wall. The most southerly peak, Spidean Coinich, is steep to the north and south but throws out a relatively gentle ridge to the east. Between this peak and Sail Gharbh lies a big corrie that rises to Bealach a'Chornaidh, the lowest point on the main ridge, and contains a fine lochan called Lochan Bealach Cornaidh. The easiest approaches to Quinag are from this eastern side. On the south side Quinag rises directly from lovely Loch Assynt and looks huge from the A837 along the loch from Skiag Bridge to Lochinver. The mountain is bare and rocky, with no trees except on the northern side, where remnants of deciduous woodland can be found in gullies and other places inaccessible to grazing animals.

Quinag is the most northerly of the massive, terraced, dark-coloured Torridonian sandstone mountains that start in the south with Beinn Bhan of Applecross (see Walk 7) and which sit on a base of Lewisian gneiss that forms the low, undulating cnoc and lochan landscape that surrounds the peaks. The east side of the mountain is made of pale quartzite, however, which rises to the most southerly summit, square-topped Spidean Coinich, and caps the highest, Sail Gharbh. This quartzite lies at an angle, its layers dipping 20 to the east. However, it must have been near enough horizontal when laid down on top of the older Torridonian sandstone as it formed from sand deposited in shallow seas. The Torridonian sandstone is horizontal now, hence the terraced appearance of mountains formed of it, so must have been tilted to the west when the sea covered it and the quartzite sand was deposited; it then tilted back to the horizontal after the quartzite had become rock, leaving this ancient seabed at an angle. The power of earth movements presents some interesting problems! The slant of the quartzite also makes the ascent of Quinag easier than it would be if the strata were horizontal, which would make for much steeper slopes.

The name Quinag means 'a milking pail', referring to the shape of the mountain, with Spidean Coinich said to resemble the pail handle. Spidean Coinich itself means 'peak of the moss', while Sail Gharbh means 'rough heel' and Sail Gorm 'blue heel', the latter two names again referring to the shapes of the peaks, in particular the slopes falling away from the summits.

Quinag has been owned by the John Muir Trust, a conservation charity dedicated to preserving wild land, since the autumn of 2005. The Trust intends to survey the mountain and produce a plan for its conservation, in particular the regeneration and spread of the native woodland.

The round of Quinag's summits is a superb walk over interesting terrain with excellent views all around. Throughout, Suilven, Canisp, Stac Pollaidh and other peaks are in view, while away to the west lies the Atlantic Ocean. The ascent is easier than it looks, Quinag being a softer mountain than it appears from below, at least on the east side, where the dip in the quartzite provides a slanting platform. Note, though, that quartzite, a hard, angular, shiny rock, is slippery when wet and much of the walk is on this rock.

The walk starts at the high point of the A894 Skiag Bridge to Kylesku road where there is a parking area **1**. Ignore the path heading north-west and head just south of west across boggy ground to the broad east ridge of Spidean Coinich **2**. Climb this ridge, mostly on bare quartzite, passing over a minor top before reaching the summit. The lower sections of quartzite are Pipe Rock, which is white in colour and has a distinctive pockmarked surface. The indentations are the ends of the burrows of worms that lived in the white sand sediments that formed the rock when this land was a marine beach some 500 million years ago. As you approach the summit, there are many big quartzite boulders that have to be crossed. The summit itself is covered with blocks of quartzite. The presence of these blocks shows that the top of the peak was not glaciated during the last ice age as the ice would have removed the loose rock. Spidean Coinich was a nunatak, a rock peak that protruded out of the ice, as was Sail Gharbh.

From 2,506-foot (764-metre) Spidean Coinich descend north-west along a narrow ridge to a minor top and then the Bealach a'Cornaidh at 1,870 feet (570 metres). On Torridonian sandstone now climb north to an unnamed 2,444-foot (745-metre) top **A**. Although only a minor summit, without enough elevation separating it from the surrounding terrain to give it much distinction, this is an important

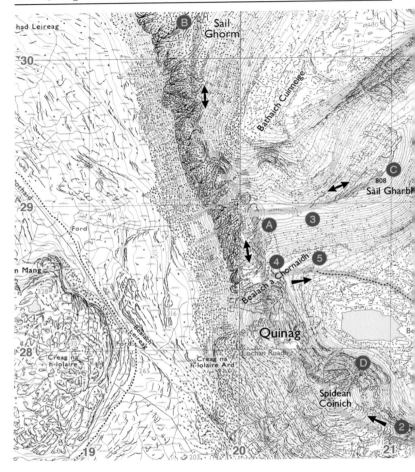

point, as it is from here that the three ridges of Quinag radiate to the higher, more dramatic tops. Continue north from this top, descending slightly and then ascending a gradually widening rocky ridge to 2,545-foot (776-metre) Sail Gorm, with the cliffs of the west face to your left. From the top **B** you can look over the depths of Bathaich Cuinneige to the sandstone buttresses of Sail Gharbh and north-west to the sea at Eddrachillis Bay. Return to the 2,444-foot (745-metre) top and turn east down grassy slopes to a col covered with flat sandstone slabs **3**. From the col easily angled slopes rise to 2,650-foot (808-metre) Sail Gharbh **C**. There are dramatic views south across Lochan Bealach Cornaidh to the dark sandstone cliffs on the north side of Spidean Coinich, with the pale quartzite summit above them.

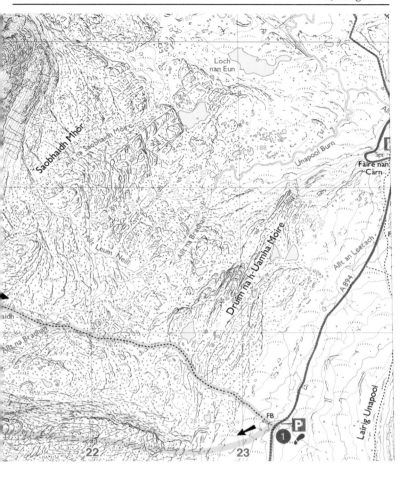

Return to the 2,444-foot (745-metre) top again, then back down to the Bealach a'Cornaidh, from where you can descend west **4** down loose steep grass, heather and boulder slopes towards Lochan Bealach Cornaidh, soon picking up an old stalkers' path **5** that leads down into the corrie and back to the start. Pause to walk down to the lochan in its splendid situation below the huge cliffs of Spidean Coinich **D**. The many boulders dotting the corrie are evidence that it was once filled by a glacier that moved these boulders here then left them when it melted. Lower down you can see long, parallel scratches left by the glacier on quartzite slabs beside the path. These scratches were made by rocks dragged along by the ice scraping over the ground below. There are random boulders – known as glacial erratics – strewn about too.

The peaks and buttresses of Quinag viewed from Loch Bealach a'Bhuirich to the east.

The Splendid Falls of Coul

8 miles (13 km)

Eas a'Chual Aluinn – the Splendid Falls of Coul – is the highest waterfall in Britain at 656 feet (200 metres) and as impressive as the name suggests. It lies far from any road in the glen of the Abhainn an Loch Bhig, beyond the head of the fjord of Loch Glencoul. The local name for the falls is the Maiden's Tresses, which comes from the folktale of a girl who hid on the cliffs above the Abhainn an Loch Bhig rather than marry a man she didn't love. When she was discovered she threw herself over the cliffs and her long hair spread out to form the waterfall.

The falls lie on the side of the glen rather than at its head and were formed when a glacier cut through an already existing river channel and gouged out the deep glen, leaving the stream to crash down the newly formed cliffs.

Eas a'Chual Aluinn can be reached by an interesting and exciting walk that runs through wild, rough country. The route starts at a parking area on the A894 south of Kylesku, near the north end of Loch na Gainmhich **1,** with the ramparts of Quinag (see Walk 16) rising to the west. From the road an old stalkers' path heads down to the loch and crosses the outlet, the Allt Chranaidh, on stepping stones above a deep, narrow ravine into which it pours in a fine waterfall. This is worth a short detour **A**. The walls of the ravine are quartzite, down which the stream tumbles 100 feet (30 metres). It is known as the Wailing Widow Fall, and it too has a sad folktale attached to it. In this story a widow and her son live alone at Kylesku, where they run a ferry and find food by hunting and fishing. However, the son is killed by a stag that tosses him into the ravine. Finding his body at the foot of the falls, his mother weeps over it as a violent storm breaks out. The heavy rain brings down a torrent of water that collapses the rock below the fall, burying the woman under it. A prominent buttress in the centre of the waterfall is said to look like the woman.

From the outlet, the path makes a traversing ascent of the slopes north-east of Loch na Gainmhich and then continues south-east above the Allt Loch Bealach a'Bhuirich to the loch itself, which is set in a rugged bowl with a small cliff at the eastern end **B**. There is a fine view west over the loch to Quinag, here seen as a range of peaks curving round a big deep corrie. The long, bare, rocky ridge that rises to the south is Glas Bheinn (the grey hill, after the pale quartzite that makes up much of the summit ridge and southern slopes). Just east of the loch the path rises to the Bealach a'Bhuirich (pass of roaring) at 1,509 feet (460 metres). This is all typical cnoc and lochan landscape – the low rocky knolls and scattered pools found wherever Lewisian gneiss forms the rock. The stony path now crosses tangled, complex rocky terrain as it descends gently to the stream that feeds the Eas a'Chual Aluinn and then follows this to the top of the cliffs where the water crashes over the edge **C**.

It isn't possible to see the whole of the falls from the edge of the cliffs, only the top section. The best view is just to the south-east, where you can see the fine tracery of water from the side, with the glen, a classic U-shaped, steep-sided, glaciated valley, stretching out beyond it to Loch Beag and Loch Glencoul. Across the glen you can see the Stack of Glencoul, a great block made of a strange metamorphic rock called mylonite, which formed due to extreme deformation at the edge of the Moine Thrust (see Introduction, pages 16–17), which runs round the front of the hill.

To see the falls in full you need to descend to the glen. The slopes around the falls are steep and rocky without a safe way down; however, there is a surprisingly easy way down not far to the south-east. A rough path heads off in this direction along the top of the crags **2**, then peters out. Continue the same way past the rocks to where the hillside opens out and you can walk down broad slopes into the glen **3**. The falls are hidden by the big buttress you have just avoided and lie just over 400 yards (0.5 km) down the glen, which at this point is quite narrow, with steep walls closing in on either side. Rough terrain leads to where the glen widens out and the falls can be seen – a long thin line of water tumbling down the cliffs **D**.

Although the tallest waterfall in Britain, Eas a'Chual Aluinn isn't the biggest in volume, carrying nowhere near the amount of water of the Falls of Glomach (see Walk 5). This is because it drains a much smaller area and its feeder stream has only seven tributaries, whereas that of the Falls of Glomach has twenty. According to Louis Stott (*The Waterfalls of Scotland*), Eas a'Chual Aluinn discharges around 250 litres per second, the Falls of Glomach 1,600 litres per second. Both pale in volume beside the Falls of Kirkaig below Suilven (see Walk 15), which discharges 7,000 litres per second. What is impressive about Eas a'Chual Aluinn, however, is its height and the wild setting. Many big waterfalls are in enclosed ravines, but Eas a'Chual Aluinn is on an open mountainside, visible from afar, and its full height can really be appreciated.

The easiest way back to the start is to climb back up to the top of the falls and return the same way. More interesting but much more strenuous is the walk down to the glen, alongside Loch Beag and over the shoulder of Cnoc na Criege. The glen floor and the loch side are both rough, with many tussocks and stones. The scenery is superlative, however, with wild, rocky slopes rising on either side. The feel is of being high in the hills, so it is a surprise to reach Loch Beag (which is really the head of Loch Glencoul) and smell the sea and see terns flying over the water.

Although rough, the going along the loch shore isn't difficult until you reach a group of islands where the loch narrows. Here the cliffs of Tom na Toine fall into the sea and the only route is a precarious narrow path high above the water. Rather than taking this route,

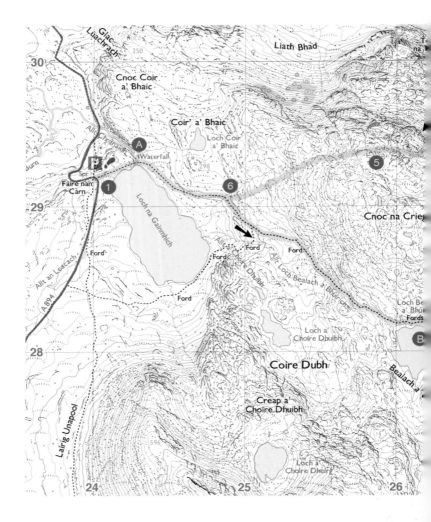

climb the steep slopes north of the ravine of the Allt a'Chnoic some 400 yards (0.5 km) before Tom na Toine **4**. The ascent is arduous but a route can be picked out through the broken crags. There are superb views back down to the loch and along the glen to the Stack of Glencoul. Once above the crags, at a height of around 1,560 feet (475 metres), contour round the north-west end of Cnoc na Criege **5** and then descend south-west to join the outward path above Loch Gainmhich **6**. From the slopes of Cnoc na Criege, Foinaven can be seen to the north and Suilven to the south, with Quinag dominant to the west (see Walks 18, 15 and 16).

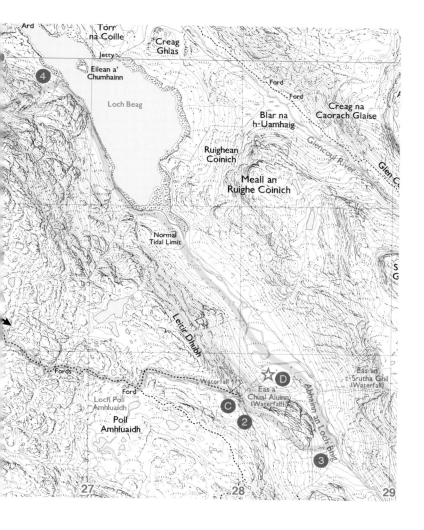

Eas a'Chual Aluinn, the highest waterfall in Britain, crashes down the open hillside. In the distance can be seen Loch Beag and Loch Glencoul.

Foinaven

14 miles (22 km)

Foinaven is a magnificent mountain in the far north of Sutherland, one of the last big hills before Scotland falls away into the sea. It lies east of the A838 Lairg to Durness road, which makes a huge dog-leg to the west to avoid Foinaven and its smaller neighbour Arkle. To the road, Foinaven presents a long, unbroken wall of steep scree that looks rather forbidding and featureless, but the eastern side above Strath Dionard is splendid, with four long, steep, rocky spurs jutting out between deep, crag-rimmed corries. Foinaven is a massive mountain, stretching some 5 miles (8 km) in a north-north-westerly direction over five summits, the highest one of which, 2,998-foot (914-metre) Ganu Mor, lies near the northern end.

Rising from an undulating landscape of low rocky hills, bogs and pools, Foinaven is a distinctive mountain. It is formed of white quartzite, the brightness of which is in sharp contrast to the dull browns and greens of the land below. The Moine Thrust (see Introduction, pages 16–17) runs across the lower eastern slopes, so Foinaven is right in the heart of a violent ancient geological upheaval. The Foinaven quartzite is 500 million years old, but it is surrounded by much older rocks. To the west, the lower rocks are 3-billion-year-old Lewisian gneiss; to the east, 1-billion-year-old Moine schists, the rocks that make up most of the Highlands. Unlike peaks further south, Foinaven is not an isolated mountain; other big hills lie to the north and south, and lower ones to the east. Indeed, Foinaven is the northern end of a line of mountains stretching for over 15 miles (24 km). East of Foinaven is a deep glen – Strath Dionard – with steep walls on the far side. Only on the west does Foinaven rise abruptly from a wide expanse of low ground – a typical Lewisian gneiss cnoc and lochan landscape.

Foinaven is a lovely, rolling word. Unfortunately it translates as 'wart mountain', the name coming from three of the summits, which have a stubby appearance. Ganu Mor means 'big head', from the Gaelic 'ceann mòr'.

The traverse of the mountain, from just outside Achfary in the south to Gualin House in the north, is one of the finest walks in the North-west Highlands – a long, adventurous undertaking in wild country. The finish is 15 miles (24 km) by road from the start, however. A combination of a car and the daily post-bus (Durness to Lairg) makes the walk feasible if you don't have a car to leave at either end. Leave the car at Gualin House, hail the post-bus and take it to the start. The steep, rocky slopes of Foinaven can only be ascended easily in a few places and this is a committing walk. A shorter option is to climb to the summit and return the same way, which is best done from Gualin House.

The walk starts half a mile (1 km) north of the little village of Achfary on the A838, where an estate track heads east across a river **1**. Cars can be parked a short way down this road. Immediately above to the north-west rise the steep slopes of Ben Stack (steep hill), which is formed of Lewisian gneiss, while to the north rise the much paler quartzite slopes of Arkle (ark hill). Take the track which runs north-east past the head of Loch Stack for almost 2 miles (3 km) to a group of buildings at Lone and another river crossing. Across the river take the left of two footpaths **2**. This leads through a small conifer plantation, zig-zags up the hillside and enters the Allt Horn glen on the southern slopes of Arkle, which it then follows up to the Bealach Horn (pass of the eagle) at 1,673 feet (510 metres) **A**.

North of the pass the broad southern slopes of Foinaven stretch upwards. Climb these to an unnamed summit just above 2,500 feet (770 metres) **B**. The slope isn't steep and if you stay east of the crest at its western edge there is grass most of the way. Foinaven itself is hidden

Foinaven from the north near the finish of the walk at Gualin House.

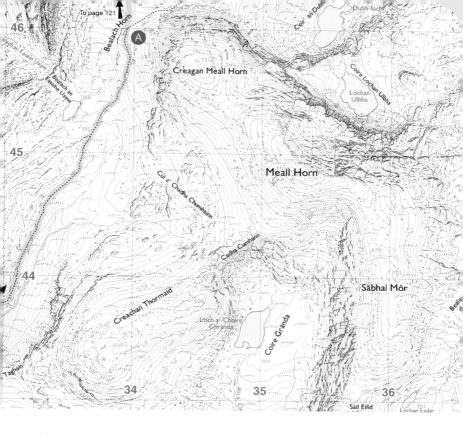

To page 121

until the minor summit is reached, when the view comes as a revelation with the peaks and corries of the mountain stretching out to the north. Masses of scree are visible, along with some bigger cliffs. Follow the ridge easily round to another unnamed summit with a spot height of 2,650 feet (808 metres), then abruptly down very steep stony slopes to Cadha na Beucaich **C**. An equally steep and stony ascent leads up a narrow ridge, above the big cliffs forming the headwall of Coire na Lurgainn, to another minor summit at 2,850 feet (869 metres). Although steep and rough, there are no real difficulties during this section, just an occasional spot where you might want to put a hand on the rock. Beyond this summit the going is easier, as the ridge broadens as it crosses another minor summit then climbs to Ganu Mor **D**.

From the summit the great sweep of the far north-west can be seen – a wonderful wild vista with a real sense of remoteness and the splendour of nature. Great mountains run away to the south – Quinag, Suilven, Canisp, Cul Mor, Conival, Ben More Assynt and, on the far horizon, An Teallach south of Ullapool. To the east the northernmost Munro, Ben Hope, looks dramatic – a steep, cliff-rimmed mountain.

From page 121

To its south Ben Klibreck rises, big and lonely. A mass of sparkling lochans stretches across low moorland to sea lochs and the coast. The golden sands of Sandwood Bay shine away to the north-west (see Walk 20). To the north lie the hill of Cranstackie and long Loch Eriboll stretching inland from the ocean.

From the summit follow the ridge round to the last summit, 2,958-foot (902-metre) Ceann Garbh, which has massive cliffs on its eastern side. Descend north-eastwards to the Bealach nan Carn then turn north-westwards to round the crags of Cnoc a'Mhadaidh **3**. Care needs to be taken on this descent, as not all the crags are obvious from above. Once out on the open, featureless moor, head north for just over 2 miles (3.5 km) over bogs and tussocks and past many lochans to the A838 at Gualin House.

To page 120

Cnoc na
Mhadaidh

Cnoc a' Mhadaidh

Bealach nan Càrn ③

Allt Coire Dùail

Ceann Garbh

Glas-Choire
Granda

Coire Dùail

Cnoc Dùail

Càrn Ⓓ
Ganu Mòr

Bràigh a' Choire Leacaich

Am Bàthaich

Foinaven or
Foinne Bheinn

A' Ch'eir Ghorm

Coire na Lurgainn

Creag Ghlas
Pollan Dhughaill

Cadha na Beucaich

Pollan
Dhughaill

Lochan na
Pollan Dhughaill

Ⓒ

An t-Sàil

Ⓑ

Glas-choire na Beucaich

Coir a' Chruiteir

Clach phoill

och nam Blàr-loch
or Loch na Tuadh

Loch na Tuadh

From page 119

31   32   33   34

Ben Loyal

11 miles (17 km)

Often described as the 'Queen of the Highlands', Ben Loyal is a beautiful mountain rising in isolation south of the Kyle of Tongue and west of Loch Loyal in the remote far north of Caithness. The castellated north-west face of the mountain is one of Scotland's classic mountain views. Four rugged peaks rise above steep buttresses divided by deep corries with a fringe of forest at their base, forming a satisfying and harmonious whole. This vista is seen well from the

The north-west face of Ben Loyal towers over the fields of Ribigill Farm.

roads around the Kyle of Tongue, especially the A838 causeway across the kyle. From the south and east rather plain, more uniform slopes rise to the summit.

Ben Loyal's distinctive shape is unlike any of the other mountains of the far north-west of Scotland. The reason is that it is not formed of quartzite or sandstone, but a rather uncommon igneous rock similar to granite called syenite, making this the only volcanic mountain in the area. When weathered, syenite forms rocky tors and buttresses like those found on granite hills much further south. Ben Loyal rises abruptly from low, flat moorland, giving it a dramatic stature that belies its 2,506-foot (764-metre) height.

The name 'Loyal' has nothing to do with loyalty, but in fact is an anglicisation of a Gaelic word, itself derived from Norse, meaning 'law'. The highest summit is called An Caisteal – the castle.

Ben Loyal lies south of the pleasant little village of Tongue, which has good facilities and is the base for the best route up the mountain.

An Caisteal, the highest summit on Ben Loyal, after a May snowstorm.

This starts 1.25 miles (2 km) south of Tongue on the minor road that runs round the head of the Kyle of Tongue **1**. A track runs south from the road here to the farm of Ribigill, with Ben Loyal rising enticingly ahead. From the farm continue towards the mountain on a muddy track through fenced cattle fields and then over boggy moorland, with the ruin of Cunside to the east. The path becomes indistinct in the marshy ground, but the way ahead is clear as you continue south towards the gap of the Bealach Clais nan Ceap, which separates the grand rock pyramid of Sgor Chaonasaid, the easternmost of the high summits of Ben Loyal, from the knobbly outlier Ben Hiel. The path becomes more obvious again and climbs beside a stream to the long, flat pass. Leave the path here **2** and climb west up steep slopes of grass, moss and heather to the ridge south of Sgor Chaonasaid **A**. As you reach the ridge, a great fang of rock appears to the south-west. This is An Caisteal. Turn right along the broad ridge **3** and ascend the rocky slopes of 2,322-foot (708-metre) Sgor Chaonasaid. Some easy scrambling is required to reach the topmost rocks, though these can be bypassed.

From Sgor Chaonasaid there is a splendid high-level walk over Ben Loyal's summits. First comes the little twin tors of 2,322-foot (708-metre) Sgor a'Bhatain (peak of the boats), from where An Caisteal appears as a square, steep-sided block of rock. Easy ground between the peaks leads to an ascent up low ledges and flat slabs on the north-west side of An Caisteal. The top is marked by a stone trig. point **B** and affords extensive views over a spacious landscape of moors, lochs and low hills. To the west Ben Hope, the most northerly Munro, looks impressive, while to the south Ben Klibreck forms a big whaleback. Northwards, the broad Kyle of Tongue stretches out to the open waters of the Atlantic Ocean. Eastwards the land is flatter and lower, the great expanse of the pool-and-stream-laced Flow Country.

Due to the crags rimming the summit, it is best to descend the same way, then cut below the rocks on the west side and continue south to the next top, 2,440-foot (744-metre) Beinn Bheag (little hill), from where there is a good view back to the south face of An Caisteal, which looks impregnable. From Beinn Bheag **4** turn west and then north, round the head of Calbhach Coire, and over an unnamed 2,138-foot (652-metre) top to the rocky summit of 2,112-foot (644-metre) Sgor a'Chleirich (cleric's peak) **C**, from which the steep, cliff-rimmed west wall of Calbhach Coire, topped by Sgor a'Bhatain, An Caisteal and Beinn Bheag, looks daunting and impressive. Sgor a'Chleirich is the top of one of the great prows of Ben Loyal and there are steep cliffs on all sides. A rocky scramble can be made with care down the north ridge, but it is much easier to return to the col **5** south of the summit of Sgor a'Chleirich and then descend steep grass into Calbhach Coire, where there is a small lochan.

The corrie is wonderfully wild, with a feeling of being enclosed in the mountains. Sgor a'Bhatain looks particularly impressive from the mouth of the corrie – a great buttress of rock towering above. Calbhach Coire is a hanging valley with steep slopes at its lip, which are most easily descended on the left (west) side of the outlet stream **5**, which drops down a steep-sided ravine. Initially the descent is down eroded black peat bogs and wobbly grassy tussocks, then rakes of grass and moss that are a little more stable underfoot. The steepness eases off just above the lovely old birch woods of Coille na Cuile **D**, which run in a long strip along the north-west and west feet of the mountain. Once in the trees, cross the stream and head north on a descending traverse **6**. The ancient woods feel gentle and sheltered after the harshness and exposure of the mountain above. In spring and summer they are alive with birdsong and flowers. The trees are festooned with mosses and lichens, and the boughs of the oldest trees are twisted and gnarled.

Below the woods you reach the open moor and there is a splendid view of the rock towers of Sgor a'Chleirich, Sgor a'Bhatain and Sgor Chaonasaid. Head north-east across the moor **7** to the outward path back to Ribigill and the start.

Kyle of

Sand

Caisteal Bharraich

Sch
Hotel
Kirkiboll PO
Tongue
FB
NTL

An Garbh-
chnoc
126   100
Rhian
Cottage

6

Rhyst

Deanside

Spr

Rhian
Bridge

Water
Spr
Creagan a'
Chàirn
100

Cairn

Ardachaidh

Coill' Ardachaidh

Mon

Creag an t-
Tràlghean

Ard Mhathain

Scrabster
(remains of)

Hut Circle

Quarry
(dis)
60

5

Garbh Chnoc

Ribigill

Hut Circles
Hut Circle

4

Rhian Burn

Lochan
na Cuilce

Coille
ri Truail

53

Lochan Hakel

Ruighean
an Daimh

Grianan
Cup & Ring
marked Rock

Feulsaid
Hut
Circl

Carn Fhada

Alt Cula Mhaillinn

Bad Salach

Hut
Circle

To page 127

57   58   59

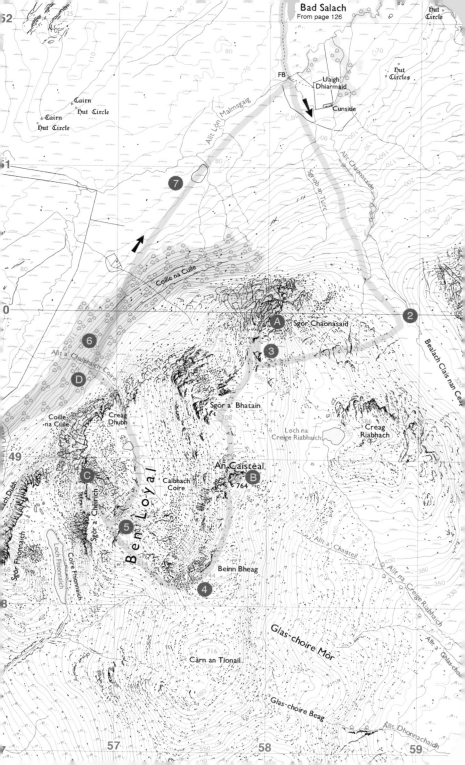

Coastal scenery between Sandwood Bay and Cape Wrath.

Sandwood Bay and Cape Wrath

12 miles (19 km)

Cape Wrath, the far north-west corner of the British mainland, is wonderfully wild and remote. The coastline around the cape is spectacular, with huge cliffs, tottering sea stacks, wave-lashed skerries, hidden coves, pebble beaches and the constant scream of seabirds. The jewel in this magnificent coast is Sandwood Bay, a curving sweep of over a mile (2 km) of pink-hued sand, backed by big sand dunes and flanked by big cliffs. Without doubt Sandwood Bay, which is owned by the John Muir Trust, is the most outstanding beach in Britain. Just inland is big freshwater Sandwood Loch.

The walk from Sandwood Bay to Cape Wrath is one of the great coastal walks of the British Isles. The remoteness and inaccessibility make it a very special trip, one to savour and relish.

The walking isn't hard, but there are some streams that could be difficult to cross after heavy rain (points 4, 5 and 6), in which case returning to the start via the outward route would be the safest option.

Depending on the exact route taken, the distance from Sandwood Bay to Cape Wrath is between 12 and 16 miles (19–26 km). A combination of buses can be used to link the start and finish. Indeed, a bus must be used at the Cape Wrath end, as there is no access for private vehicles. In the south, daily buses (run by Tim Dearman Coaches) between Ullapool and Durness stop at Kinlochbervie, which is 3 miles (5 km) from Blairmore, the closest you can get by road to Sandwood Bay. A minibus service links Cape Wrath with the Kyle of Durness and a passenger ferry to the east shore about a mile south of Durness. This service runs between May and September and is dependent on the weather. It's wise to phone as close to your trip as possible to check times (01971 511343/287). The area inland from Cape Wrath is a naval gunnery range. Sentries are stationed and red warning flags flown when firing takes place to ensure that walkers don't stray into danger areas. This doesn't affect the route as described here. Shops and other facilities can be found in Kinlochbervie and Durness.

From the car park at Blairmore **1** an old track runs north-east across boggy peat moorland to Loch na Gainimh then north to Loch a'Mhuillin, where it becomes a footpath **2** that runs past Loch

Meadhonach and Loch Clais nan Coinneal to Sandwood Bay. The total distance from Blairmore to Sandwood Bay is 3.5 miles (6 km). The first view of Sandwood Bay comes from a rise above Sandwood Loch **A**: a superb view north across the bay to distant cliffs. The wild setting and the great expanse of sand running down to the crashing surf is an exciting and inspiring sight. The path ends at the edge of the sand **B**. To the south-west a ragged tower of rock rises out of the sea, the sea stack known as Am Buachaille (the herdsman). The sea can look tempting on a hot summer's day, but swimming is inadvisable due to strong currents and undertow. Behind the marram-grass-dotted sand dunes is a stretch of machair – beautiful shell-sand grassland that is covered with flowers in spring and which provides good grazing for the sheep of local crofters. The machair between Sandwood Bay and Oldshoremore is some of the finest on the mainland, most machair being found on the western coasts of the

Sandwood Bay and the sea stack of Am Buachaille.

Outer Hebrides. The area around Sandwood Bay is mostly Torridonian sandstone, a rock that forms huge vertical cliffs but which also erodes in spectacular and unusual formations.

Sandwood sounds English, but in fact comes from the Gaelic 'sandabhat', meaning 'sandy water', the 'bhat' (pronounced 'vat') itself derived from the Norse 'vatn', meaning water. The bay has a peaceful, lonely feel; a sense of real remoteness. Unsurprisingly perhaps, there are many legends associated with it, including stories of the ghost of a sailor haunting the cottage whose ruins stand above the west shore of Sandwood Loch, and tales of Spanish gold buried in the bay from the wreck of a galleon from the Spanish Armada. Mermaids are said to come here too.

The walk continues across the sand, with an easy ford of the short outlet stream from Sandwood Loch, to the northern end of the bay, from where there is an easy climb on to the cliffs **3**. From here to

Cape Wrath is a breathtaking and exciting walk – a wonderland of sea stacks, caves, coves, arches, deep tidal ravines known as geos, blow-holes, crumbling sandstone ledges and cliff after cliff, rising and falling, rising and falling, with the thundering sea always just beyond. Waves break on the rocks, spout up through the geos and boom in the depths of the caves. The highest cliffs are 295 feet (90 metres) above the sea, giving dizzying views down into the surging waves. There is no footpath, though plenty of sheep tracks, but the terrain is mostly grassy and the going relatively easy. Some small rivers have to be crossed – the Strath Chailleach stream **4**, the Keisgaig River **5** and the Allt na Clais Leobairnich **6**; these could be difficult or even impossible to ford when in spate, but aren't usually a problem.

Prolific birdlife accompanies the whole walk and birdwatchers will be delighted, while even those who usually ignore birds will find it hard to do so here. Just inland from the coast moorland birds such as wheatears, skylarks and golden plovers can be seen, while the coast has oystercatchers, cormorants, shags, gulls, terns, fulmars, guillemots, razorbills, puffins, gannets, great skuas, kittiwakes and more. Divers are found on both the ocean and the lochs, and ravens wheel over the cliffs and the inland moors.

About half a mile (1 km) before Cape Wrath two impressive sea stacks appear – A'Chailleach (the old woman) and Am Bodach (the old man) **C**. Such stacks are formed when arches collapse in the middle, leaving the seaward part standing alone. Eroded constantly by the sea, the stacks themselves will eventually crumble and collapse.

Not far beyond the sea stacks lies Cape Wrath, marked by a lighthouse that has been in view for many hours **D** and some other buildings. This lighthouse was built in 1828 by Robert Stevenson of the famous 'Lighthouse Stevensons' family, grandfather of Robert Louis Stevenson, author of *Treasure Island*, *Kidnapped* and *Dr Jekyll and Mr Hyde*. Before the lighthouse was erected many ships were wrecked on this treacherous rocky coast. Once manned, it is now automated.

The name Wrath is Norse in origin and derives from 'hvarf', meaning a headland. It is a major feature on sea routes and was important for the Vikings, as it was here that they rounded the northern coast of Scotland and headed towards their homes in Scandinavia. Of course a cape is a headland (from the Latin for head), so Cape Wrath is really Cape Cape. The only other cape in Britain is Cape Cornwall in the far south-west of England.

The cliffs at Cape Wrath are as dramatic as those further south and time waiting for the minibus can be spent gazing down them to the Atlantic waves and watching the many seabirds.

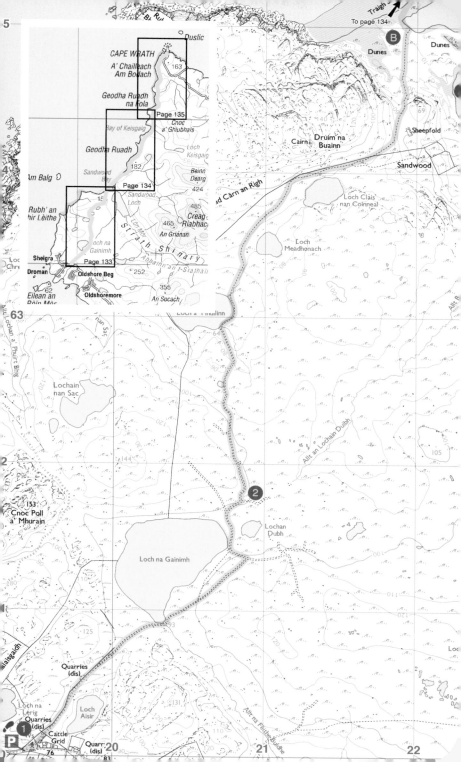

Duslic

CAPE WRATH
A' Chailleach
Am Bodach

Geodha Ruadh
na Fola

163

Page 135

Cnoc
a' Ghiubhais

Bay of Keisgaig

Geodha Ruadh

Loch
Keisgaig

Sandwood
Bay

182

Beinn
Dearg

424

Page 134

Sandwood
Loch

Am Balg

Rubh' an
hir Lèithe

15

485

Creag
Riabhach

465

An Grianan

Strath Shinary

och na
Gainimh

Sheigra
Droman

Oldshore Beg

252

Abhainn an t-Srathain

Page 133

62

Oldshoremore

Eilean an
Ròin Mòr

355

An Socach

To page 134

B

Dunes

Dunes

Loch

Traigh

69

Sheepfold

Cairn

Druim na
Buainn

Sandwood

ud Carn an Rìgh

Loch Clais
nan Coinneal

Loch
Meadhonach

63

Loch a' Fhridhinn

nan Sac

Allt an Lochain Dubh

105

Lochain
nan Sac

100

120

144

2

153

Cnoc Poll
a' Mhurain

Lochan
Dubh

280

Loch na Gainimh

100

110

125

193

120

Quarries
(dis)

131

alasgaidh

Loch na
Lerig

Loch
Aisir

110

Quarries
(dis)

1

P

Cattle
Grid

Quarries
(dis)

76

83

Allt na Fèithe Buidhe

Loc

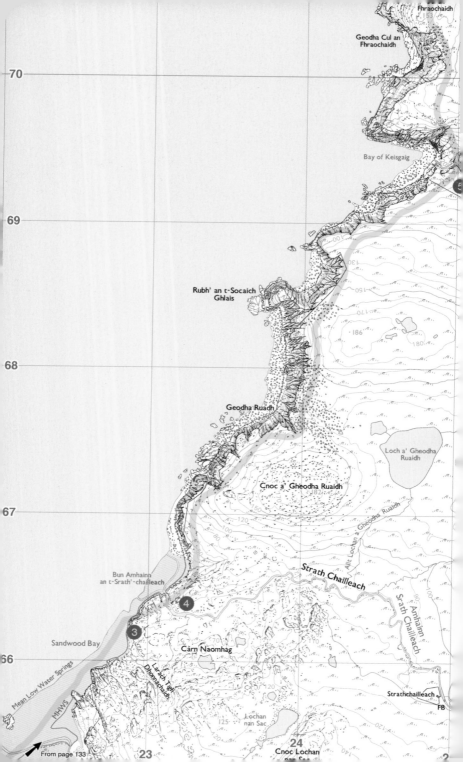

Fhraochaidh

Geodha Cul an
Fhraochaidh

70

Bay of Keisgaig

69

Rubh' an t-Socaich
Ghlais

68

Geodha Ruadh

Loch a' Gheodha
Ruaidh

Cnoc a' Gheodha Ruaidh

67

Strath Chailleach

Bun Amhainn
an t-Srath'-chailleach

4

3

Sandwood Bay

Carn Naomhag

Larach Tigh
Dhonnachaidh

Strathchailleach

FB

66

Lochan
nan Sac

From page 133

23

24

Cnoc Lochan

☆ Cape Wrath

Stac an Dùnain   Natural Arch

Acairseid Choinnich Oig

Geodha an Fhuarain

The small rocky Island of Duslic is situated 1 km NE of Cape Wrath

Uamh Chàm (Cave)

D

Dùnan Mòr

163

Geodha Glas

Cave

A' Chailleach

Am Bodach

C

Clais Charnach

Clais an Dùnain

Old Shielings

44

Dùnan Beag

81

Allt na Clais Leobairnich

Clais Leobairnich

6

170

Goedha Ruadh na Fola

Cul an Fhraochaidh

Geodha Cul an Fhraochaidh

Sithean na h-Iolaireich

Cnoc a' Ghiubhais

75

74

73

72

71

25   26   27

Marsco

8 miles (13 km)

The Red Hills is the name given to the striking group of steep-sided, rounded hills that dominates the landscape between Broadford and Sligachan on the north-eastern coast in the southern half of the Isle of Skye. The name comes from the pale pinkish granite from which the hills are formed, which contrasts with the dark rocks of the mountains lying to the south and west – the rugged Cuillin. Both groups of hills are the remnants of volcanoes that erupted around 55 million years ago when the Caledonian mountain range was splitting apart and the Atlantic Ocean starting to fill the gap forming between Europe and North America. The final appearance of the hills was formed during the ice ages, when they were sculpted by glaciers and meltwater. The Cuillin are rock mountains with very narrow ridges, pointed summits and many cliffs. To climb them requires a head for heights, good scrambling skills and in a few cases rock-climbing ability. The Red Hills are softer and gentler, with broader ridges and few cliffs; they are much more suited to the walker who doesn't want to grapple with rocks perched over sheer drops.

Marsco lies in the Western Red Hills close to the Cuillin. It is on the east side of Glen Sligachan and is isolated from other hills, making it a superb viewpoint. It stands out in views down Glen Sligachan from the A87 and the Sligachan Hotel, appearing as an almost symmetrical pyramid. The bulge on the western side is a crag called Fiaclan Dearg (red tooth). The combination of its shape and its dramatic situation makes it the finest of the Red Hills. The summit is 2,414 feet (736 metres) high. The name is Norse and means 'seagull hill'.

The Sligachan Hotel played a part in the history of Scottish mountaineering, as many early climbers who pioneered routes in the Cuillin stayed here. As well as bars and hotel rooms, it has a bunkhouse and there is a campsite nearby. The nearest shops are in Broadford, south along the coast, and Portree, north along the coast. Buses from Fort William to Portree stop at Sligachan. Although Marsco looks fine, the view at Sligachan is dominated by the great scree cone of Glamaig to the east and spiky Sgurr nan Gillean at the northern end of the Cuillin ridge to the south.

The ascent of Marsco begins at the A87 bridge over the River Sligachan **1**, where there is a car park. Take the path through a gate in a fence above the old bridge, which lies south of the new one, where a signpost points to Loch Coruisk (see Walk 22). The path runs along the side of the glen, above the boggy ground beside the river. Marsco grows in stature as you walk down the glen towards it. After 2 miles (3 km) the path reaches a side stream, the Allt na Measarroch, and a path junction **2**. Leave the main path here and follow the rough, boggy and sometimes indistinct path beside the Allt na Measarroch up the long, narrow glen called Coire Dubh Measarroch to the broad 935-foot (285-metre) pass of Mam a'Phobuill **A**, which lies between Marsco and Beinn Dearg Mheadhonach. Mam a'Phobuill means 'pass of the people'

View down Glen Sligachan to Marsco near the start of the walk.

and is said to have been used by Bonnie Prince Charlie when hiding from government troops after his defeat at the Battle of Culloden in 1745; the pass connects Glen Sligachan with the head of Loch Ainort and is an easy way through the Red Hills. 'Mam' means 'breast' and is often used for a broad pass like this, probably because it resembles the dip between two breasts, rather than 'bealach', which is usually a narrower, steeper pass. Looking east from the pass there are splendid views of Bla Bheinn, Garbh-bheinn and Belig – rocky hills that are outliers of the Cuillin. Marsco rises south of the pass, massive and steep, with a corrie called Coire nan Laogh (corrie of the calves) hollowed out of its flanks. The ascent of Marsco makes a circuit of this corrie.

From the Mam a'Phobuill cross the stream running out of Coire nan Laogh **3**. This runs in a narrow, rocky channel and tumbles into a ravine in a roaring waterfall that can be heard during the ascent in quiet weather. A line of old fenceposts leads the way up the east side of the corrie **4**. Although steep in places, the going on scree, heather and grass isn't hard and the south-east ridge of Marsco is soon reached at a shallow dip. Turn north-west here **5** and climb the ridge, which is quite narrow but not exposed, to the little summit, on which there is a small cairn **B**.

The narrow summit ridge is a superb viewpoint, one of the best in the Scottish hills, and a place to linger and absorb the wild beauty rather than leave quickly. Dominating the view to the south and west is the Cuillin ridge, a dark, jagged line of summits curving round Harta Corrie; it looks magnificent, intimidating and thrilling. To the south, over the pale pink screes of little Ruadh Stac (red peak), Loch na Creithach fills the deep glen of Srath na Creithach, which separates the main Cuillin from Bla Bheinn and the other outliers. Beyond the loch lies the grassy meadow and pebble beach of Camasunary, fronting the open sea of Loch Scavaig with the islands of Rum and Eigg in the distance. East of Loch na Creithach, Bla Bheinn rises as a steep, bulky rock mountain fractured by many gullies, Garbh-bheinn as a smoother-sided peak with a short summit ridge above a dark corrie. Turning northwards, the Red Hills look smooth and simple in contrast to the shattered, ragged Cuillin, with Glamaig a solid lump rising behind the more elegant pyramid of Beinn Dearg Mhor.

Descend from the summit on stony ground to the northern arm of Coire nan Laogh **6**, which is rough, stony and steep before it becomes grassy, and descend this back to the Mam a'Phobuill and the outward path back to Sligachan.

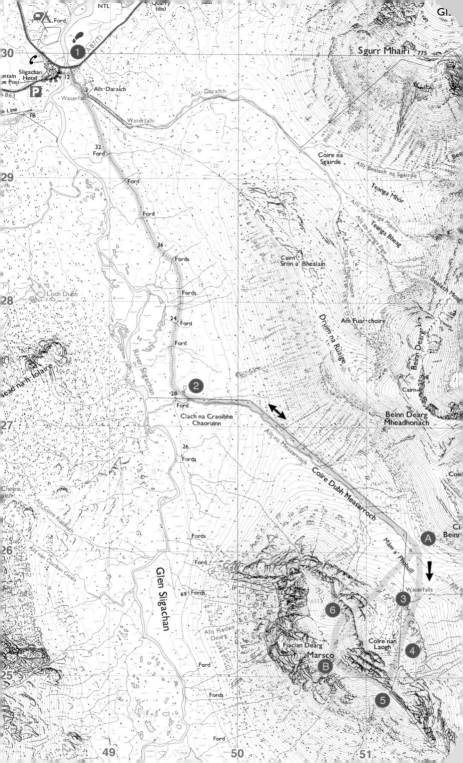

Loch Coruisk and the Elgol Coast Walk

6 miles (10 km)

The Cuillin are the most spectacular mountain range in Britain, a magnificent arc of splintered rock peaks with an amazing array of pinnacles, cliffs, corries and arêtes. At the heart of the Cuillin lies Loch Coruisk, a wild sheet of water in a deep corrie right below the Cuillin summits and the most impressive place in the British hills.

A classic viewpoint for the Cuillin is Elgol, an attractive little village at the mouth of Loch Scavaig on the west side of the Strathaird peninsula, which lies on the south side of the Isle of Skye. This walk runs from Loch Coruisk to Elgol on land owned and protected by the John Muir Trust. Elgol is at the end of a very long dead-end road that runs round the head of Loch Slapin from Broadford, from where it can be reached by post-bus. Most of the walking is rough but not difficult. However, there are two potential problems.

Right at the start, the Scavaig River has to be crossed, which can be impossible after heavy rain. Then on the coast between Loch Coruisk and Camasunary a rock slab called the Bad Step has to be crossed. Whilst this isn't difficult, it is exposed and best not attempted by anyone with a poor head for heights or who is unsure of their balance.

The classic, and most interesting and scenic, way to reach Loch Coruisk is by sea, which can be done from Elgol on the *Bella Jane*, a wonderful 45-minute boat ride. This is the way the first visitors came, including luminaries such as the author Sir Walter Scott and the painter J. M. W. Turner, and it is still, in my view, the best way. From Coruisk a path, rough in places, leads round the coast back to Elgol. The boat journey crosses Loch Scavaig to a landing-stage consisting of iron steps in a rock slab in inner Loch na Cuilce, passing en route an island on which seals bask and with good views south to the rocky peaks of the island of Rum. From the landing-stage **1** it is just 400 yards along the Scavaig River, one of the world's shortest rivers, from the sea to the freshwater of Loch Coruisk and one of the world's greatest views **A**. From the loch the Cuillin rise up, a rock wonderland of enormous variety curving round the loch.

Coruisk runs north-west, walled on the northern side by a long subsidiary rocky ridge of the Cuillin called Druim nan Ramh (ridge of the oars). Ringing the head of the corrie are the long ridges and summits of Sgurr a'Mhadaidh (peak of the fox) and Sgurr a'Ghreadaidh (peak of torment), then along the south-east side are ranged Sgurr na Banachdich (milkmaid's peak), Sgurr Dearg (red peak), Sgurr Mhic Choinnich (Mackenzie's Peak), Sgurr Dubh Mor (big black peak), Sgurr nan Eag (peak of the notches) and Gars-bheinn (echoing mountain). On top of Sgurr Dearg a blade of rock can be clearly seen. This is the famous, or perhaps infamous, Inaccessible Pinnacle, the hardest Munro of all, as rock-climbing skills are needed to ascend its steep, narrow ridge. The Cuillin are built of gabbro, a very rough, dark volcanic rock that is excellent for rock climbing.

Coruisk means 'corrie of water', from the Gaelic 'Coir'Uisg', and as well as the loch there are masses of little streams which very quickly turn into raging torrents after heavy rain. It was carved out by glaciers during the ice age. Cuillin probably comes from the Norse 'kjolen', which means 'high rocks' – a plain, accurate description.

The Scavaig River, which runs down a series of slabs into Loch Scavaig, can be crossed on stepping stones where it leaves Loch Coruisk. If the stepping stones are awash with water, then returning to the landing stage and taking the boat back to Elgol is a good idea. Once across the stepping stones, take the path up the east side of the loch 400 yards (0.5 km) or so for the best views of the Cuillin. Return to the Scavaig River and take the rocky path heading south-east **2**. This cuts across the neck of the little peninsula of Rubha Port Sgaile to the coast at Loch nan Leachd then follows the shore of Loch Scavaig

Camasunary Bay and the coast to Elgol.

round the foot of the little, though exceptionally rugged and rocky, hill called Sgurr na Stri (hill of strife) to Camasunary Bay.

The walk is rough and rocky, but not difficult except for the short crossing of one huge cracked slab of rock called the Bad Step **3**, which runs down into the sea, blocking the way. Negotiating the Bad Step involves an easy scramble, starting with a narrow ledge that leads up to a tiny platform from which you balance along the edge of a wide crack in the slab, hands on the rock, back down to sea level amongst some big boulders. From the Bad Step the path continues close to the sea with excellent views south to the islands of Rum and Eigg. It crosses the neck

of the point of Rudha Buidhe, then reaches Rudha Ban and turns north-east along the west side of Camasunary Bay (Camas Fhionnairigh – the bay of the fair shieling). The Cuillin ridge is hidden now, but a superb view opens up of Bla Bheinn (the blue mountain) in the north-east.

When you reach the head of the bay you cross a river, the Abhainn Camas Fhionnairigh **4**. The mouth of the river is tidal and it can be forded here at low tide. If the water is too deep, go upstream a few hundred yards to where it is shallower. In prolonged wet weather finding a safe place to ford can be difficult. Once across the river you are for the first time in this walk on gentle terrain – a beautiful sward of green turf above a sloping stony beach **B**. At the west end of the bay is a small open bothy, at the east end a locked estate house. Soaring above this lovely relaxing spot is the long, rocky south ridge of Bla Bheinn.

Another river runs into the bay at its east end: the Abhainn nan Leac. This too can be forded easily at low tide. At other times there's a bridge **5** a few hundred yards inland where a wide track from Camasunary to the road down the east side of the Strathaird peninsula crosses the river. Across the river take the path running south along the rocky coast that stretches out into the distance. Easy walking not far above the sea leads to the point of Rubha na h-Airighe Baine **6**, where the path climbs into a scattered narrow stretch of pretty deciduous woodland – oak, birch, holly, hazel, aspen – on the steep lower slopes of Beinn Leacach (hill of the bare rock).

From the trees the path descends to the grassy meadows of Glen Scaladal, with the cliff of Carn Mor (big rock) on the slopes of Ben Cleat (hill of the cliff) rising ahead. Across the mouth of the glen the path traverses the steep hillside below Ben Cleat just above the sea, then rises to pass below Bidein an Fhithich (peak of the raven) and run through some fenced fields to a vehicle track that leads to the upper of the two car parks on the steep road running through the stretched-out little village of Elgol. There are superb views of the Cuillin back across Loch Scavaig throughout the walk from Camasunary to Elgol.

South Duirinish and Moonen Bay Coastal Walk

14 miles (23 km)

Skye is famous for its spectacular mountains. Far less well known is its coastline, yet the far western coast of the Duirinish peninsula on Skye is the most magnificent in Britain, arguably equalled only by that from Sandwood Bay to Cape Wrath on the mainland (see walk 20). The reason for the relative neglect of this coast is undoubtedly its remoteness, along with the lack of any public transport, making a linear walk awkward unless you have two cars (or perhaps a car and a bicycle) and can leave one at the end of the walk.

The walk described here runs along the South Duirinish Coast, which is a wonderland of cliffs, arches, stacks, geos (sea-filled ravines) and caves, to the great curve of Moonen Bay, where the cliffs are unbroken for many miles and rise to almost 1,000 feet (300 metres). The cliffs are built of basalt, a volcanic rock, and are the edges of the massive lava flows that cover northern Skye.

The walk starts at Orbost House **1**, where there is space for parking. It lies on a minor road forming a loop south of the A863 Sligachan to Dunvegan road. The nearest town with all facilities is Dunvegan. From Orbost House a track runs south to Loch Bharcasaig, an inlet of big Loch Bracadale, which separates Duirinish from the Minginish peninsula. The track follows the shoreline, with good views of Loch Bracadale and the surrounding gently undulating countryside, to a wooden bridge across the Abhainn Bhearscaig. Beyond the bridge the track enters a large conifer plantation, which stretches for several miles down the coast, and runs through the trees across the hillside well above Loch Bracadale. At Forse Burn **2** the track becomes a path and splits. Take the right-hand of the two paths, which runs south through the trees to a pass **A** between two low hills, Beinn na Moine and Beinn na Boineid, with a good view of the island of Rum to the south and the cliffs of northern Minginish across Loch Bracadale.

The path drops a little from the pass to cross a stile over a fence and runs above little Brandarsaig Bay. The ruins of an old stone shieling and some modern metal sheep pens lie next to the path, just before the shallow Brandarsaig Burn is crossed by a pretty little waterfall bordered by rowans and aspens **3**. After this brief interlude, the path returns to the conifers until the edge of the forest is reached at the Idrigill Burn **4**, across which lie the remains of the old village of Idrigill and some still visible lazybeds – a cultivation method in which crops were grown on rows of raised earth.

From Idrigill the path crosses a mix of heather moorland, dense patches of bracken and cropped sheep pasture, and passes between two low hills, Ard Beag and Steineval. The many sheep tracks in this area can be confusing, but the terrain is gentle and all you need do is walk south to the coast. As you do so a superb vista suddenly opens up as the sea appears with the three sea stacks of MacLeod's Maidens

Waterfall and natural arch at Lorgasdal Bay, South Duirinish.

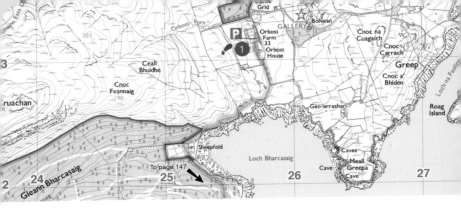

just off the coast **B**. A legend about these stacks says that a Norse goddess called Ran and her maidens are imprisoned in them as punishment for capturing the spirits of sailors from ships wrecked by Ran's husband Oegir, who caused the storms that sank the ships. In the form of the stacks Ran and her attendants still lure boats to disaster – obviously a reflection of the dangers of sailing along this rocky coast. The highest stack, known as the Mother, is 230 feet (70 metres) high; the two lower stacks are known as the Daughters. Care is needed when viewing Macleod's Maidens from the cliff top, as the edge is crumbling and dangerous. The best view of them is half a mile (1 km) further west across the little bay of Inbhir a'Gharraidh.

From the south-western end of this bay **5** the walk follows the coast north-westwards, with wonderful views throughout. There are many paths, mostly sheep tracks, across the close-cropped turf. As well as the grand coastal scenery there are masses of seabirds – fulmars, gannets, kittiwakes, guillemots, razorbills, puffins, gulls, terns, cormorants, shags and more – whose wild cries fill the air and add to the atmosphere of remoteness and natural grandeur.

After rounding Inbhir a'Gharraidh the walk crosses the lower slopes of Ben Idrigill. The coastline opens up and you can see all the way along the coast to The Hoe near the end of the walk. The path descends into a series of glens that run down to the top of the cliffs, then rises again to the headlands between them. The cliffs at the end of the first of these glens, Glen Lorgasdal **C**, have some of the finest views of the whole walk, with sea stacks, pinnacles, an arch and a fine waterfall tumbling down the cliffs. Next comes Glen Ollisdal, then Glen Dibidal **D**, where the River Dibidal crashes into the deep ravine of the Geodha Mor in another impressive waterfall, forcing you to head inland a few hundred yards **6** in order to cross it safely.

The next section of coast is replete with caves and arches. Particularly outstanding is the big deep arch in the headland north of

the stream draining Loch an Fhridhein. North of this is an unusual, long, tunnel-like arch. Next comes Scaladal Burn, which has cut back into the coast to form a long, narrow ravine into which it slips in two long, thin waterfalls **E**. To cross the burn, head inland a few hundred yards to where you can easily descend to it **7**. On the far side climb up on to the cliffs of Biod Boidheach, then descend to sea level – for the first time since the start of the walk – at Lorgill Bay **F**. Here there are green pastures, a little burn, some low walls and old fields, the last remnants of a crofting community that was evicted in 1830 in the notorious Clearances, when landowners removed people from the land, often forcibly, to make way for sheep.

Above Lorgill Bay is The Hoe, a rounded 764-foot (233-metre) summit **G** set back a few hundred metres from the cliff edge. The steepest climb of the walk leads to the top **8**, rewarded by the splendid vista. The whole of Moonen Bay can be seen – a great curve of cliffs running round to Waterstein Head and Neist Point. Eastwards, the distinctive flat-topped pair of hills known as Macleod's Tables rise from undulating moorland, while away to the south the jagged silhouette of the Cuillin ridge can be seen.

The cliffs rimming The Hoe are massive and the slowly descending walk along them gives marvellous views as you cross the headland of Hoe Rape and then drop down to Ramasaig Bay **H**, where you can walk down to the beach. This is a lovely, restful spot and a fine end to the walk along the cliffs. A little waterfall splashes down on to the shore, and to the north rises the broad green grass slopes of the southern end of Ramasaig Cliff. Those with energy can continue up this cliff and on round Moonen Bay to Waterstein Head. Most, however, will turn inland and walk the 400 yards (0.5 km) beside the stream to Ramasaig, a lonely house at the end of a long road running south from Glendale. Cars can be parked near the house.

The Quiraing

7 miles (11 km)

Trotternish is the northernmost peninsula on Skye and contains the strangest and most unusual landscapes on an island full of the strange and unusual. The Trotternish Ridge is a 23-mile- (37-km)-long escarpment running almost the whole length of the peninsula, with a gentle dip slope to the east and a steep scarp slope on the west. Along this scarp slope are many landslips giving rise to weird and otherworldly rock formations. The reason for these landslides is that the basalt rock that covers the surface here – the solidified outpourings of lava from many volcanoes – lies on weaker sedimentary rocks that have given way under the weight of the basalt, causing it to slip down the hillside.

The most bizarre and extraordinary result of these landslides is the Quiraing, a tangled mass of eroded pinnacles, towers and buttresses lying below Meall na Suiramach at the northern end of the Trotternish Ridge. Exploring the Quiraing is entertaining and can be combined with an ascent of the northernmost hills on Skye. 'Quiraing' is a curious word for a curious place. However, it probably just means 'pillared enclosure' – an apt if prosaic description – from the Gaelic 'cuith raing'.

The Prison rock formation.

The walk to the Quiraing starts at the high point on the Staffin to Uig road, the only one to cross the Trotternish Ridge, where there is a car park. Buses run to Staffin 3 miles (5 km) away, but there is no public transport to the start of the walk. Staffin has a café too. All facilities can be found in Uig.

Cross the road from the car park to a path **1** that heads north-west across the steep hillside below cliffs towards the first Quiraing formations, just a mile (1.5 km) away. The path is narrow and thrilling, giving the impression of entering a different world. To the west are views over moorland to the neat fields of coastal crofts and the sea. The first hint of what is to come is a rugged hummock on the hillside some way below the path; this is Cnoc a'Mheirlich ('hillock of the robber').

The Quiraing **A** is a mysterious, hidden place in which you can wander through the tangle of peculiar formations cut off from the world outside. Many of the formations are distinctive enough to have names of their own. The first of these is on the right of the path, cutting off the view of the sea and marking entry to this eccentric and, in mist, eerie place. This first formation is a long slice of rock with a spiny crest called the Prison, which presents vertical rock to the path and steep grass to the sea. You can scramble along the Prison but you need a good head for heights and the rock is rotten and loose in places. A 118-foot (36-metre) overhanging spire called the Needle rises above the Prison uphill from the path. Amazingly, this tottering pinnacle has been climbed.

Leave the main path here and take a side one that runs behind the Needle, up a gully and between rock buttresses into the depths of the Quiraing. Strange rock formations, many with flat grassy tops, are all around. The biggest of these is appropriately called the Table **B**, a huge edifice which can be ascended in several places, the easiest being on the landward (east) side. The flat green top is a splendid place to relax amidst the grotesque and twisted rocks.

On the seaward side, steep slopes drop to open lochan- and landslip-dotted moorland. To the east a wall of rock prevents access to the Trotternish Ridge. To find a way through the cliffs and reach the ridge, return to the main path and follow it north below the Quiraing, then along the base of the cliffs **2**, ignoring the sheep tracks and paths descending to the right. Ahead you can see flat-topped Leac nan Fionn, another landslip formation, below the slopes of Sron Vourlinn, the northernmost peak on the Trotternish Ridge.

At a junction where a path cuts right to run below Leac nan Fionn **3** keep heading north under the crags into the complex terrain of the landslip between Sron Vourlinn and Leac nan Fionn, to where the narrow path climbs steeply through a breach in the rocks to reach another path on the ridge above, a spur of the main Trotternish Ridge, at Fir Bhreugach **4**. Now above the cliffs, turn right on this path and walk the short distance along their edge to the 1,246-foot (380-metre) summit of Sron Vourlinn **C**. There is a tremendous, spacious view over the sea and the many islands of the Hebrides. Rubha Hunish, the most northerly point on Skye, can be seen, while to the east broken crags rim Sgurr Mor (big peak) across Coire Mhic Eachainn.

Turn back from Sron Vourlinn and follow the path towards Meall na Suiramach, with wonderful views over the ragged Quiraing and out to Staffin Bay and the sea. Before reaching the summit turn north again **5** and ascend the easy-angled grassy slopes of 1,620-foot (494-metre) Sgurr Mor for more views of the north end of Skye and the spreading sea. The walking all along the Trotternish Ridge is mostly on close-cropped grass and is generally easy.

From the summit head back south to the trig. point on 1,781-foot (543-metre) Meall na Suiramach **D**. The summit is a broad, gentle dome, giving no hint of the chaotic landscape just a few hundred yards away. In poor visibility it's best to follow the broad south-east ridge of Meall na Suiramach over Maoladh Mor down to the road. When clear, though, it is far more enjoyable to follow the edge of the cliffs **6** and look down on the labyrinth of the Quiraing. To the south the landslip of

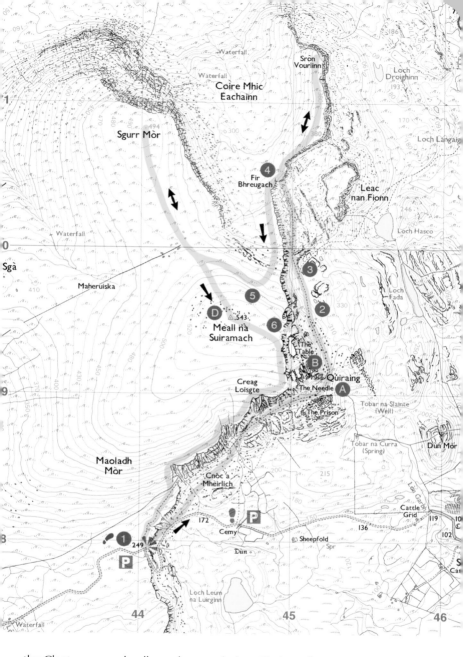

the Cleat, a craggy knoll, can be seen below Biod Buidhe. Beyond this summit the ridge undulates southwards to a distant but distinctive pinnacle called the Storr. The slopes start to steepen just above the road, but the walk down to it is easy.

USEFUL
INFORMATION

The National Trust for Scotland

Wemyss House, 28 Charlotte Square, Edinburgh EH2 4ET
   tel. +44(0)131 243 9300; fax +44(0)131 243 9301
   email information@nts.org.uk; Website www.nts.org.uk

NTS Properties in the North-west Highlands

Glenfinnan Monument: NTS Information Centre, Glenfinnan,
   Highland PH37 4LT
   tel./fax 01397 722250; email glenfinnan@nts.org.uk
Balmacara Estate & Lochalsh Woodland Garden: Lochalsh House
   (NTS), Balmacara, Kyle, Ross-shire IV40 8DN
   tel. (01599) 566325; fax 01599 566359
   email balmacara@nts.org.uk
   Ranger/naturalist: tel. 01599 511231
   website www.nts-seabirds.org.uk
Corrieshalloch Gorge National Nature Reserve: Braemore, Ross-shire
   Managed from Inverewe Garden, tel. 01445 781200; fax 01445
   781497; email inverewe@nts.org.uk Countryside office: tel. 01445
   712622
Falls of Glomach: Ross-shire: Ranger Service: tel. 01599 511231
Inverewe Garden: Poolewe, Ross-shire IV22 2LG; tel. 01445 781200;
   fax 01445 781497; email inverewe@nts.org.uk
   Countryside office: tel. 01445 712622
Kintail & Morvich: Morvich Farm, Inverinate, Kyle, Ross-shire IV40 8HQ
   tel. 01599 511231
Strome Castle: Ross-shire
   tel. 01599 566325; fax (01599) 566359
Torridon: The Mains, Torridon, Achnasheen, Ross-shire IV22 2EZ
   tel./fax 01445 791368
West Affric: Ross-shire; tel./fax 01599 511231

North-west Highlands Geo Park

www.north-west-highlands-geopark.org.uk

Accommodation

Mountain Bothies Association: www.mountainbothies.org.uk
Scottish Independent Hostels: www.hostel-scotland.co.uk
Scottish Youth Hostels: 01786 891 400, www.syha.org.uk
Stilwell's (campsites): 01305 250151, www.stilwell.co.uk
The Camping and Caravanning Club: 024 7669 4995;
   www.campingandcaravanningclub.co.uk
UK Camp Site: www.ukcampsite.co.uk

Transport

Trains

National Rail Enquiries: 08457 48 49 50; www.nationalrail.co.uk
First ScotRail: 08700 005151; www.firstscotrail.com

Buses

Cape Wrath Minibus Service: 01971 511343/287;
    www.capewrath.org.uk
National Express: 08705 808080; www.nationalexpress.com
Royal Mail Post-buses: 0845 7740740; www.royalmail.com
Scottish Citylink: 08705 505050; www.citylink.co.uk
Tim Dearman Coaches: 01349 883585;
    www.timdearmancoaches.co.uk
Traveline Scotland: 0870 608 2 608; www.travelinescotland.com
UK Bus Timetable Website Directory:
    http://timetables.showbus.co.uk/
Lochaber Transport Forum: c/o The Highland Council Roads and
    Transport Services, Lochy Bridge Depot, Carr's Corner Industrial
    Estate, Fort William, PH33 6TL; tel: 01397 709 011; fax: 01397
    705 735; www.lochabertransport.org.uk/

Ferries

Caledonian MacBrayne: 08705 65000; www.calmac.co.uk
Arnisdale Ferry Service: mbm1@mailcity.com;
    www.arnisdaleferryservice.com; 01599 522774, 01599 522352
    Murray Morrison, The Doune, Glenelg, By Kyle, Ross-shire IV40 8LA
Bella Jane Boat Trips (Skye): 0800 731 3089; www.bellajane.co.uk
Corran Ferry, Lochaber Transport Forum: c/o The Highland Council
    Roads and Transport Services, Lochy Bridge Depot, Carr's Corner
    Industrial Estate, Fort William PH33 6TL
    tel. 01397 709 011; fax 01397 705 735
    www.lochabertransport.org.uk/corranferry.html

Tourist Information Centres

Scottish Tourist Board: 0845 22 55 121; www.visitscotland.com

Bettyhill
Brora
Durness
Fort William
Gairloch
Kinlochbervie
Lairg

Lochinver
Mallaig
Strathcarron
Strontian
Tongue
Ullapool

Weather forecasts

Weather and Avalanche Information
Met Office West Highland Forecast:
www.metoffice.gov.uk/loutdoor/mountainsafety/westhighland.html
Metcheck Mountain:
www.metcheck.com/mountain
Mountain Weather Information Service North-west Highlands:
www.mwis.org.uk/forecast.php?area=1s
AccuWeather.com:
ukie.accuweather.com/adcbin/ukie/ukie_mountain_index.asp
BBC Radio Scotland 92-95fm, 810mw:
Outdoor Conditions Forecast:
19.12 Monday–Friday (following the 19.00 news bulletin)
18.55 Saturday; 20.00 Sunday

Further reading

Beinn Eighe: The Mountain above the Wood: the story of the first fifty years of Britain's first National Nature Reserve, J. Laughton Johnston and Dick Balharry (Birlinn, 2001).

Exploring the Far North West of Scotland: a walker's guide to the hills, glens and coastlines of Wester Ross and Sutherland, Richard Gilbert (Cordee, 1994).

Exploring the Landscape of Assynt: a walkers' guide and map showing the rocks and landscape of Assynt and Inverpolly, Kathryn Goodenough, Elizabeth Pickett, Maarten Krabbendam and Tom Bradwell (British Geological Survey, 2004).

Highways and Byways in the West Highlands, Seton Gordon (Birlinn, 1995; first published 1935).

Hostile Habitats: Scotland's Mountain Environment: a hillwalker's guide to wildlife and landscape, ed. Nick Kempe and Mark Wrightman (SMT, 2006).

Hutton's Arse: 3 billion years of extraordinary geology in Scotland's Northern Highlands, Malcolm Rider (Rider-French, 2005).

Isle of Skye Rambler's Guide, Chris Townsend (Collins, 2001).

North to the Cape: a trek from Fort William to Cape Wrath, Denis Brook and Phil Hinchcliffe (Cicerone Press, 1999).

North-west Highlands: a landscape fashioned by geology, John Mendum, Jon Merritt and Alan McKirdy (Scottish Natural Heritage, 2001).

North-West Highlands: Scottish Mountaineering Club Hillwalkers' Guide, Dave Broadhead, Alec Keith and Ted Maden (SMC, 2004).

Scottish Hill and Mountain Names, Peter Drummond (SMT, 1991).

The Backpacker's Handbook, Chris Townsend (Ragged Mountain Press, 2005).

The Cape Wrath Trail: a new 200-mile walking route through the North-West Scottish Highlands, David Patterson (Peak Publishing, 1996).

The Highland Geology Trail, John L. Roberts (Luath Press, 1998).

The Waterfalls of Scotland, Louis Stott (Aberdeen University Press, 1987).

Torridon, the nature of the place, Chris Lowe (Wester Ross Net, 2003).

Glossary of Gaelic and Scots words

The maps of the North-west Highlands are full of Gaelic and Scots names whose meanings will be unknown to non-speakers of those languages. Understanding the names adds to comprehension of the culture and landscape. Here are some of the more common words you will come across.

Aber, abhair mouth of a river, confluence
Abhainn river
Achadh (ach, auch) field, meadow
Airde (ard) height
Airidh, airigh mountain pasture, shieling
Allt stream
Aonach ridge
Ath ford
Bac bank
Bad place
Baile township
Ban, bhan white, fair
Beag (beg) small
Bealach pass
Beinn hill or mountain
Beith birch tree
Ben hill or mountain, anglicisation of Gaelic beinn
Bidean (bidein) peak
Binnein conical top
Biod pointed top
Bo, ba cow, cattle
Bodach old man
Bothy hut, shelter

Braigh (brae) hill, heights
Breac speckled
Buachaille herdsman
Buidhe yellow
Buiridh (bhuiridh) roaring of stags
Burn stream
Cadha steep slope, pass
Cailleach old woman
Caisteal castle, fort
Cam crooked
Camas (camus) bay
Caol (kyle) narrows
Caor rowan
Carn hill, pile of stones (cairn)
Cas steep
Cat wild cat
Cean (ceann, ken, kin) head
Choinneach mossy place, marsh
Cioch (pl. ciche) breast
Cir comb
Ciste chest
Clach stone

Clais narrow valley, gap
Cleit cliff
Cnap (cnoc) hillock
Coille wood
Coire corrie, cirque, hollow
Craobh tree
Creachan rock
Creag crag, cliff
Croit croft
Cruach heap or stack
Cul back
Da two
Dail field
Damh deer
Darach oakwood
Dearg red
Diollaid saddle, pass
Diridh divide
Doire copse, wood
Drochaid bridge
Drum (druim) ridge
Dubh dark, black
Each horse
Eag notch
Eagach notched
Eaglais church
Eas waterfall

Eighe file, notched
Eilean island
Eun (eoin) bird, birds
Fada (fhada) long
Fas level
Fear man
Fearna alder
Feith bog, moss
Fionn white, bright
Fraoch heather
Fuar cold
Fuaran spring, well
Gabhar goat
Gaoth wind
Garbh rough, stony
Geal white
Gearr short
Giuthas Scots pine
Glac hollow
Glais stream
Glas (ghlas) grey or green
Gleann (glen) valley
Gorm blue
Inbhir (inver) river mouth
Innis (innse) island or meadow
Iolair eagle
Ladhar hoof, fork
Lag (lagg, lagan) hollow
Lair mare
Lairig pass
Laogh (laoigh) calf
Lax salmon
Leac stone, slab
Learg slope
Leathad slope

Leis lee, leeward
Leitir steep slope
Liath grey
Linne pool
Loch lake
Lochan small lake
Lub (luib) bend
Machair seaside meadow
Maighdean (mhaighdean) maiden
Mairg rust coloured
Mam rounded hill, pass
Maol bald head
Meadhon (mheadhoin) middle
Meall hill
Moine moss, bog
Monadh mountain
Mor (mhor, more) big
Muillin (Mhuillin) mill
Muc (muic) pig
Mullach summit
Ness point or headland
Odhar dun coloured
Ord rounded hill
Poite pot
Poll pool, pit
Raineach ferny
Rath fort
Righ (ree) king
Ros headland
Ruadh red
Rubha (rhu) coastal headland

Ruigh shieling
Sail heel
Saighead arrow
Saobhaidh animal's den
Sgiath wing
Sgurr (sgorr) rocky peak
Sith fairy
Sithean fairy hill
Sloc (slochd) hollow
Sneachd snow
Socach snout
Spidean peak
Sput (sputan) spout
Srath (strath) broad valley
Sron nose
Stac steep rock
Steall waterfall
Stob peak
Stuc peak, steep rock
Suidhe s eat
Tairbert (tarbert) isthmus
Tarmachan ptarmigan
Teallach forge, hearth
Tigh house
Toll hollow
Tom hill
Torc bear
Torr small hill
Traigh beach
Uaine green
Uamh cave
Uig bay
Uisge water
Vik bay, creek